Sweet

Aroma

The Unhindered Power of the Believer

by

Liz Todd

Sweet Aroma
Copyright © 2001 by Liz Todd
ALL RIGHTS RESERVED

Fairmont Books is a ministry of The McDougal Foundation, Inc., a Maryland nonprofit corporation dedicated to spreading the Gospel of the Lord Jesus Christ to as many people as possible in the shortest time possible.

Published by:

Fairmont Books
P.O. Box 3595
Hagerstown, MD 21742-3595
www.mcdougal.org

ISBN 1-58158-031-2

Printed in the United States of America
For Worldwide Distribution

Dedication

To the glory of His name.

To all those in the Body of Christ who are hungry
for more of God.

About the Cover

If I were to distill what I believe to be the essence of this book, I would say that it is symbolized in the cover. The design was not of my choosing. As I sought the Lord in prayer one morning, this cover design flashed before my eyes in the form of a picture. As I focused on what I was seeing, I was given an understanding of the symbolism the cover portrays.

The red color represents the blood covenant of Jesus Christ that we are called to walk in. The white writing symbolizes the purity and righteousness God is bringing the Church into. The upside-down drawing of a church building depicts the process I sense God is about to begin. The fact that it is a child's drawing speaks of the simple, uncomplicated faith of a child that we are called to have. When we walk in covenant relationship with the Lord, in purity and righteousness, in childlike dependence upon our heavenly Father, then our lives will be a *Sweet Aroma*, an acceptable sacrifice, pleasing to our Lord Jesus.

Acknowledgments

I would like to thank my daughters, Sarah, Angie and Laura, for their encouragement and support and for allowing me to use their stories.

I would also like to thank my husband, Geoff, for being generous in giving me time and space to write and travel.

Thank you to my prayer partners, Gail Poyser, Anne Wright and Graeme Macdonald, for your friendship and faithful prayer support.

To my friend and mentor, Robyn Heath, thanks for all the late-night phone calls.

Thanks to all those friends and family members who gave me permission to use their testimonies. May the stories enrich the lives of many.

To Bill Gurney, the first Christian therapist I had the priviledge of observing and working with. Thank you for showing me how it's done. You were a good role model and mentor. Many thanks.

I would also like to thank Dr. Sim Choo Jek of Resurrection Life Ministries, for his encouragement and support and for making himself available to the Lord. He is a father in the faith.

Finally, I am grateful to the staff at McDougal Publishing for their wise counsel throughout the publishing process. Many thanks for sharing your God-given talents.

Contents

"I will accept you as a SWEET AROMA when I bring you out from the peoples and gather you out of the countries where you have been scattered; and I will be hallowed in you before the Gentiles."

Ezekiel 20:41, NKJ

Introduction

The Church is in a state of transition. God is changing us both individually and corporately, and what is emerging has been described by some church leaders as "a new apostolic reformation." To enable us to embrace these changes, we need to be released from every barrier that would hinder God's purposes in our lives.

God is turning us upside down. He is changing our values so that we, the Church, can individually and corporately reflect the love of God to the world. Apostles are "sent ones," and God wants to send a whole generation of believers into the world to be "as Jesus." He was the expression of God's love to humanity, and this new move of God is about us, the Church, being prepared now by the Holy Spirit to be the expression of that love.

Part of our preparation involves coming to an understanding of the things in our lives which may hinder the flow of God's Spirit. This book is partly about exposing some of those areas which may act as blockages, so we can take action to remove them. The book also presents foundational biblical principles we need to know and understand to be able to successfully take hold of the freedom Christ offers us.

The extent to which we understand the victory we have in Christ will dictate the extent to which we are able to walk in that victory. Through the use of practical examples — in the form of testimonies from both my own life and the lives of others — I have endeavored to demonstrate what we can expect to happen when God moves to bring us to wholeness and then releases us to serve Him.

There is a paradigm shift going on in Christendom, and in these early stages, we don't yet fully know what God has in store for us. But one thing we *do* know: God is bringing together a Body unified by love.

Having worked in the field of counseling for thirty years, the last ten of those years specifically with Christians from various denominational backgrounds, I have come to see a widespread need across the Body of Christ. That need is to understand the ways of God in leading us into our spiritual potential. My purpose in writing this book is to suggest some broad guidelines, or biblical principles, involved in emotional and spiritual healing — particularly where there are persistent problems, so that we can come into our potential, both individually and corporately.

I have learned from experience that God does a better job of changing lives than any human counselor ever could. This is saying a lot, for I met the best counselors the university I was attending had to offer during my years as a young student struggling with loneliness, depression and anxiety. It wasn't until I met Jesus, however, that I found real peace. Christ completely set me free.

As a result of experiencing the transforming power of the cross, as a young university graduate, I developed a growing longing to tell others that there is a God who is real, who loves us and who wants to heal our lives. In the years since then, I have learned that it's all about cooperating with Him. He has made it simple; we just need to understand His ways. He leads; we follow.

In Chapter Seven, I give a personal testimony of how my life was interrupted abruptly one day in May of 1998, when God's manifest presence filled my office while I was counseling. It saturated me to the point that I could not function. My life has not been the same since.

I thought I had completed writing this book after Chapter Eleven. The Lord, however, called me to a three-week "Daniel" fast, and as I neared the end of the fast, the Holy Spirit began to give me some understanding about apostolic restoration and the new apostolic leadership being raised up. He gave me progressive revelation over a period of twelve days, and at the end of the twelve days, I had Chapter Twelve. After I finished that chapter and had begun writing the Introduction, I sensed the Holy Spirit urging me to look up the symbolic meaning of certain numbers.

I was aware that God uses numbers in a meaningful way, that He has put His signature upon His creation in numbers. But I was totally unaware of a whole set of circumstances the Lord seems to have arranged, until the Holy Spirit prompted me to consider them.

Those interested in biblical numerics and the way in which God speaks through His numbering system can read in the following section how the Lord placed His hand upon the book in an unexpected way.

Likewise, in the section About the Cover, I have described how, once again, the Holy Spirit gave guidance in an unexpected way. It is my desire, first and foremost, that this book would glorify the name of Jesus and that in reading it you will long for a closer walk with Him.

Liz Todd
Brisbane, Australia

God's Numbering System

There are many Christians who believe that the Bible contains intricate numerical patterns beneath the surface of its original text. It is believed that not only the Bible, but also nature, indeed all of God's creative work, is marked, or identified, by numerical patterns. Writers such as Ivan Panin, Karl G. Sabiers, R. McCormack, M. Mahan and J. Edwin Hartnill are among those who attribute symbolic numbers to the direct revelation of God. [1]

Some scholars argue that it is only the number seven which is used symbolically in the Scriptures to an significant degree, while others believe there is extremely limited number symbolism in the Bible or none at all. Although scholars are divided in their opinion regarding this subject, I was surprised to discover some interesting circumstances surrounding the writing of this book.

As I mention in the Introduction, it came as a complete surprise when the Holy Spirit began to open up to me the interesting pattern of numbers, specifically multiples of three, surrounding the circumstances of writing the book, particularly Chapter Twelve. The Holy Spirit reminded me that He had begun to speak to me about apostolic leadership as I was seating my-self in a plane bound for Sydney. That was when He began to give me Chapter Twelve.

The number twelve represents divine government or apostolic fullness. [2] The Lord reminded me that my seat number was 12C — the twelfth row and the third seat from the window. The number three repre-sents divine completeness or perfect testimony. [3] The Lord reminded me that He stopped speaking to me about the apostolic move twelve days later at 12:30 PM on the third of June. The number thirty symbol-izes consecration and maturity for ministry. [4] Next, I was reminded that I had been in training for thirty years. June is the sixth month, and six is the number of man. [5]

After the Lord showed me all these numbers of multiples of three, He reminded me that He had called me to that three-week "Daniel" fast prior to His speaking to me. He had me check the Old Testa-ment book of Daniel, and I found that it happens to be the twenty-seventh book (three times nine equals twenty-seven), the book has twelve chapters, and I was called to a three-week fast.

Then I was reminded that it took me nine months to write the book. On the ninth day of the sixth month, I held the completed manuscript in my hand. The number nine stands for finality, fullness, fruitfulness, the number of the Holy Spirit and the number of the fruit of the womb. [6]

Eventually, I thought I had finished looking up numbers, but the Lord urged me to search for the passage in Daniel where that prophet's fast is described. It is found in the first chapter. One is the number of God, the beginning, source or commencement, [6] and the fast is described in the twelfth verse. While it is important to adhere to a sound system of hermeneutics as we interpret what God is saying to us, our God is too creative to be limited in the ways He chooses to draw our attention and show that He is with us. Truly, we serve an amazing God whose ways transcend comprehension. He is too big for us to fathom.

O Lord, have mercy on me in my anguish. My eyes are red from weeping; my health is broken from sorrow. I am pining away with grief; my years are shortened, drained away because of sadness.

Psalm 31:9, TLB

One

*

Everyone Has a Story to Tell

I was sitting at my desk writing notes when the phone rang.

"Are you Mike's counselor? I'm one of his mates at the building site. He's out on the ledge of a three-story building planning to jump. Here, you talk to him. I'm handing him the mobile phone."

Suddenly, I was bolt upright, at full attention, drawing on all my reserves. I remembered many movies I'd seen in the past where the police negotiator crept up behind some desperate individual poised on the side of a bridge and calmly convinced him that life was worth living. I had always admired these heroes and never envied their position.

I could hear Mike mumbling over the sound of the wind whistling around the top of the building. He was saying, "I've got to do it! I've got to do it! I'm going to jump!"

Summoning everything within me and realizing I might be the last person to speak to this man alive, I calmly reminded him of the contract he and I had. "Remember what we discussed in our counseling sessions. You agreed that if it ever got so bad that you actually wanted to jump, you would admit yourself to the psychiatric hospital because you believe you owe it to your wife and child to stay alive."

"Yes, I remember, but it's been so hard all day. It's all I can think about. I've got to do it!"

"That's not what you said last week. You said you wanted to stay alive to raise your child. Now, tell your workmates you're coming in off the ledge and that they are to drive you to the hospital straightaway."

With some gentle coaxing, Mike agreed, and his nervous mates bundled him into the car and headed for the hospital. Such is the face of human pain!

Over the years, I have encountered many people overwhelmed by life's tragedies. I have seen the aftermath of murder, armed robbery, gang rape, incest, war, hostage situations, family breakdown, infidelity, abandonment and rejection. The list of painful situations human beings encounter is endless, and people's lives are moulded to a large extent by these experiences. One could be tempted to be discouraged by this fact.

I'll never forget the day I was driving home from work feeling miserable, drooped over the steering wheel, reminding myself of how unfair life was. I had just come from a two-hour counseling session in which three women, a mother and her two adult daughters, each confessed, all at the same time, that they had been sexually abused, much to the shock and horror of the other two. It was also much to my own distress. I was the counselor, but I could only look on as the three women sobbed uncontrollably.

As I wallowed in my misery, the Lord gently reminded me that this was precisely why He came — to destroy the works of the devil and to bind up the brokenhearted. I was encouraged. Of course, there's hope. We do not have to remain defeated. There is every possibility for living a good life. I already knew that and was learning to live it myself, but I had temporarily taken my eyes off the facts. I was reminded that not only had Christ come to set us free, but that He is also our peace in the midst of trouble (see Philippians 4:6).

The hard part is learning to live in the peace of God while the turmoil of life surrounds us. This is something that the Lord begins to teach us from the moment we are born again, and He is determined to complete the task, if only we will allow Him to do it.

We have as our perfect model, Jesus, who slept in the back of the boat while a fierce storm raged, threatening to sink the vessel (see Matthew 8:23-27). The disciples actually had to wake Jesus up and ask Him to save them all from drowning. He seemed genuinely surprised by their level of anxiety and rebuked them for their lack of faith. If ever anyone knew how to live in the midst of turmoil, Jesus did.

The amazing peace Jesus exhibited in the midst of terror stands as testimony to the level of security He experienced in His heavenly Father. But it is our Lord's desire to bring us all to such a place of trust that we also, like Jesus, would learn to have confidence in difficult times.

The Scriptures promise that we will have trouble:

> *Dear friends, do not be surprised at the painful trial you are suffering, as though something strange were happening to you.*   1 Peter 4:12

> *In this you greatly rejoice, though now for a little while you may have had to suffer grief in all kinds of trials. These have come so that your faith — of greater worth than gold, which perishes even though refined by fire — may be proven genuine and may result in praise, glory and honor when Jesus Christ is revealed.*
>   1 Peter 1:6-7

In all these trials, God has a purpose. He is testing our faith and developing character in us. He is teaching us to depend upon Him so that He can bring us into our spiritual potential. God has good plans for us (see Jeremiah 29:11). He promises us peace in the midst of difficulty (see John 14:27) and promises never to test us to the point that we would lose our faith (see 1 Corinthians 10:13).

It is the absence of such peace that leads a person to seek counseling. Why do they come to us? Individuals will usually begin to look outside of themselves for help when they have used up all their own resources for coping, and they lack the skills required to resolve their problems. In other words, they feel helpless and, quite often, overwhelmed by their emotions.

While emotions are very real, they do not necessarily reflect the truth about a given situation. When feelings are overpowering, we tend to forget that our battle is not against people, but against the powers of darkness (see Ephesians 6:12). So often couples come to see the pastor or the counselor to get help with their marriages because they see their spouses as being difficult. And while that may be the case, over and above that is the profound truth that, as Christians, we are waging a spiritual battle. This battle is very real, and it is fierce:

> *Be self-controlled and alert. Your enemy the devil prowls around like a roaring lion looking for someone to devour. Resist him, standing firm*

> *in the faith, because you know that your broth-*
> *ers throughout the world are undergoing the*
> *same kind of sufferings.*   1 Peter 5:8-9

We know that the enemy comes to steal, to kill and to destroy (see John 10:10) and that he will take any opportunity we give him to wear us down. But obviously, if it is so simple that all we have to do is put on our armor and resist the devil, then all our problems would already be solved. Clearly, there is more to it. Coming to know Jesus Christ as Savior and even being baptized in the Holy Spirit is wonderful, but this does not necessarily resolve all our social and emotional problems.

Our struggle seems to be focused around our efforts to get basic needs met. We all need to feel loved, and we all need to feel safe. These are possibly our two most basic emotional needs, and it is amazing how creative we can become in trying to meet them.

Little children, for instance, are very resilient, and when their needs for adequate nurturing are not met, they find ways of surviving psychologically. Children who are deprived of love and security will put up walls deep within themselves as protection against the onslaught of reality. After all, it is just too painful to believe that "nobody wants me," or that "there is something radically wrong with me," "I am fundamentally flawed" or "I am really bad." It is just as frightening to realize that "no one is capable of caring for me," "life is not safe" or "I can never get enough."

Sometimes, a child is offered conditional love: "Be different, and you will be accepted." Some children are protected from ever having to make a decision or form an opinion, and they end up helpless. At other times, the unspoken messages within a family are so powerful that the child just instinctively knows that to feel or express anger is considered wicked. Such powerful conditioning in the formative years trains human beings to play games to get their needs met.

When a married couple show up for counseling and express frustration with each other, it is not so much that either of them is a bad person, but rather that conflict arises from the way they go about trying to get their needs met. They become irritated by the brokenness in their mates. This will be highlighted even more dramatically if the husband and wife have been raised in families with vastly different styles of relating.

Some families are close and affectionate, while others are more distant and cool. However, the expectations we have developed have a lot to do with our disappointments.

We may have learned to survive as children — but at a price. The kinds of psychological defenses we develop while growing up seem to work reasonably well

— until we move into intimate relationships and get married. The demands of intimate relating become our undoing, and we can no longer hide. Our survival skills now have to change, and we must adapt, or our relationships may perish.

It is not just getting married that may signal the beginning of problems for many, but sometimes other turning points in life can be very unsettling as well. Graduating from high school, starting university, becoming a parent, moving to another house, retirement, joblessness, illness and bereavement all demand adjustment. Just how flexible and adaptable we are depends a lot on what was modeled for us as children. Did our parents teach us good problem-solving skills? If not, somehow we have to make up the shortfall. Suddenly, we are faced with one of life's problems and find ourselves scrambling for a solution. Our failure to rise to the occasion may plunge us into despair. We may become overwhelmed with anxiety or feel very confused.

In our confusion, we just cannot understand why we keep repeating the same mistakes. Why can't we get on top of things? Why is there no way out? Usually, we are unaware that we see the world through our own particular rose-colored glasses and that we have adopted a view of the world that fits our experiences in life. A child born into a family of great privilege could be excused for believing: "life is easy. You can have whatever you want. You should sit back and enjoy the ride. The world is my oyster."

A child from a poverty-stricken family, on the other hand, may grow up thinking: "Life is tough. Life is unfair. You never know where your next meal is coming from, so grab all you can while you can." What about the common belief "You've got to work hard to get ahead in this life"? Many sons have followed in their fathers' footsteps and obeyed this deeply held conviction, some achieving success, to their deep satisfaction, and some not, to their great frustration.

A view of life that is relatively common, certainly in the Western world, is "Look out for number one." This attitude may come from a person's being hurt in early life and feeling "ripped off."

And on it goes. There are as many worldviews as there are people on this planet, because as we grow up and experience life, we form our opinions about reality. Let's face it, everyone has a story to tell!

What we don't realize at the time is that it is only our own reality and, therefore, represents a very subjective viewpoint. This viewpoint colors everything in life, from the way we respond to people in relationships, our expectations of ourselves and others, our plans, our dreams, our vision for the future and, probably most important, how we see God. The question is: How close is this viewpoint to God's reality? Why does that matter? In his letter to the Roman believers, Paul reminds us of the need to renew our minds:

> *Do not conform any longer to the pattern of this world, but be transformed by the renewing of your mind. Then you will be able to test and approve what God's will is — his good, pleasing and perfect will.*   Romans 12:2

We need to have our minds conformed to God's way of thinking so we can follow Him. We must allow the Holy Spirit to adjust our worldview to fit God's reality. He wants to help us learn how to stand against the popular forms of worldliness so our lives can reflect Him. So, if we find ourselves saying, "I have to be thin to be acceptable," or "I have to win to be okay" or any other of the many popular lies, we know our perspective on life needs some adjustment.

Those layers of woundedness which have so distorted our sense of reality stand as testimony to the need for change. We need to be set free, free from everything that holds us back from becoming what God intends, free to love, worship and serve God with our whole being, free to walk in victory.

It is God's love in Christ that sets us free, and once we know we're loved, we're on the road to healing.

The Lord is close to those whose hearts are breaking; he rescues those who are humbly sorry for their sins. The good man does not escape all troubles — he has them too. But the Lord helps him in each and every one.

Psalm 34:18-19, TLB

Two

❦

In Bondage, Who Me?

You've no doubt heard the saying "You are what you eat." I guess this is true to a large extent, but the Bible tells us that we are what we *think* (see Proverbs 23:7). This is a very powerful statement, because the suggestion is that our thought processes determine the outcome of our lives, influencing both our present and our future. Is it any wonder that there is a battle going on for our minds? If Satan can influence us with his lies to the point that we see the world the way he presents it, then he has won, and we have lost. At that point, we are defeated.

Since the mind is so powerful, is it any wonder that as soon as we become new creations in Christ, God tells us to renew our minds according to His Word (see Romans 12:2)? Gradually, we learn to bring every thought into captivity to Jesus Christ (see 2 Corinthians 10:5).

If we are what we think, then to a very large extent both our emotions and our behavior will be a direct result of our thoughts. So, if we want to change the way we feel and the way we do things, a good place to start is to examine how we think.

As we are growing up, we are not aware of the extent to which we develop distorted thinking. Both the spoken and unspoken messages within families deliver powerful statements regarding our importance as people. We end up feeling valued or devalued according to how we are treated, and we may end up with a distorted image of ourselves — not what God intended.

So, how do we get unstuck? How do we know if we are bound by a distorted self-image and are not seeing things the way God does? A good way to tell is to analyze what is going on when we feel stressed and unhappy.

Why are we stressed? What are we expecting of ourselves or others or of the world in general that is hard to attain? Have we set such high expectations for ourselves that if we do not perform to a certain level, we just cannot accept ourselves? Do we have "all or nothing" thinking? Perhaps we learned somewhere along the way that if we performed extremely well we would receive praise, and now we live like this automatically. If so, we are stressed because we are anxious about how others see us. We never feel settled; we are exhausted from continually extending ourselves. We live lives of striving, striving, striving. Nothing is ever good enough!

There is a very poignant story in the Bible of Leah who kept having children, hoping that her husband Jacob would be pleased and fall in love with her:

> *When the LORD saw that Leah was not loved, he opened her womb, but Rachel was barren. Leah became pregnant and gave birth to a son. She named him Reuben, for she said, "It is because the LORD has seen my misery. Surely my husband will love me now."*   Genesis 29:31-32

God made us with a need to be loved, and like Leah, we will do virtually anything to have that deep need met. We crave acceptance and approval. Without it, we are disturbed within, and we do not feel whole. Not feeling loved will lead us either to strive for love in various forms or, perhaps to just give up and stop trying altogether.

It may be that we have had a big setback and see ourselves as failures. The pain is too great to bear and depression sets in, as we feel powerless to change our circumstances. We may wonder why we experience cycles of depression, but if we analyze it, a pattern may emerge. The depression may follow a personal failure each time. This painful cycle can only be changed by correcting our distorted image of self.

Elijah slipped into depression after he realized he was incapable of bringing revival to the northern tribes of Israel. He had just seen an amazing victory, as he stood against Ahab and Jezebel, who had murdered nearly all of the Lord's prophets. God told Elijah that both he and the prophets of Baal were to build altars to the deity they each worshipped. The god who answered with fire would be acknowledged as Lord over the whole of Israel.

They built altars, then cut the sacrificial bulls into pieces and placed them on top of the wood. The prophets of Baal called on their god, but nothing happened. Elijah built a trench around his altar and poured water over the sacrifice three times — enough to fill the trench. He then called on God:

> *"Answer me, O LORD, answer me, so these people will know that you, O LORD, are God, and that you are turning their hearts back again." Then the fire of the LORD fell and burned up the sacrifice, the wood, the stones and the soil, and also licked up the water in the trench.*
>
> 1 Kings 18:37-38

After Elijah had the priests of Baal killed, he prayed, and God sent rain, bringing an end to a devastating three-year drought. God had sent both fire and rain from Heaven on the same day. Elijah had expected revival to follow these amazing events, but it did not, and instead he found himself fleeing from Jezebel, who vowed to kill him. Elijah sat exhausted under a tree and declared, *"It is enough; now, O LORD, take away my life; for I am not better than my fathers"* (1 Kings 19:4, KJV).

Elijah realized he was powerless to change circumstances. His expectations were disappointed, and discouragement followed. Depression is as old as history, and not only Elijah, but Job, Jeremiah and Jonah all record feelings of great discouragement when life did not go the way they had expected and desired.

Some Christians are hard on themselves, believing that if a person suffers from anxiety or depression, it is because that person does not have enough faith in God's Word. While there may be some truth to that, the question must be asked as to why we are finding it difficult to believe God's promises. Normally, if we have the capacity to believe, we do.

Our failure to believe usually has something to do with the fact that we have come to believe that we are unworthy, and that while God might love everyone else, He couldn't possibly love me. The Word of God is true, but not for me! The problem resides not in lack of faith in God's Word so much as in our inability to receive.

Such deep emotional wounds have taken years to become entrenched. Some people are like a puppy that is daily kicked and abused and, therefore, will cower in a corner when approached. Usually, it is because they have never known unconditional love and acceptance. It is almost impossible for them to see themselves as valuable and, therefore, worthy to receive love. They live on the defensive, constantly expecting rejection. This is the only reality they have ever known. A revelation of God's love is needed for healing to take place.

To be human means that, from time to time, we will feel anxious or depressed. These feelings might occur simply because we are tired and more vulnerable than usual. Or sometimes we can feel "down" for a few days following one of life's big changes, like getting married, having a baby or starting an important new job. After the big event has happened and all the excitement is over, our emotions just take a nosedive. It is when the symptoms do not settle down, but continue over time or keep recurring, that it is indicative of deeper underlying issues that God wants to heal.

What is important for us to realize is that not all the quirky little things we do are because of our personalities. Some of them are just ways of coping — strategies to get us through life. We can get into a rut, repeating ineffective responses to situations simply because we don't know what else to do.

It may be that we have fallen into the trap of living

like a doormat, not knowing how to set boundaries in relationships, because our need to be loved is so great. Perhaps the knowledge that someone does not like us is just too painful to bear, so we increase our efforts to please others, finding it difficult to say "no," not wanting to offend, but inwardly feeling resentful of being "put upon." This is exhausting, because people can be hard to please. We so want to be relaxed and easygoing like others, but we learned, at a very young age, that you have to please people to be accepted.

Another way of coping with the strain of not being our real selves is simply to wear a mask and pretend to be someone we are not. This method of coping when feeling threatened might actually be effective some of the time, but the truth of the matter is that the inner restlessness is still there. The peace we long for does not come.

For quite a while now, the Lord has been drawing my attention to a specific behavior in the Church that is used characteristically as a mask. This activity, widely employed across the whole Body of Christ, is plagiarism, which simply means to "take something that somebody else has written or thought and try to pass it off as original." [1]

About a year ago, I went to visit a church across town one Sunday night. They were having a visiting speaker, a well-known and well-respected pastor (who has, as far as I am aware, an unblemished record). That night, he preached a very interesting and stimulating sermon. Two days later, I walked into a Christian bookstore, went straight to a certain shelf and picked up a book. When I opened the book, there, to my amazement, was the sermon he had preached. He had preached the whole book, without one word of recognition about his source. At that moment, I realized there was a reason God was showing this to me.

God wants us to have truth in our inward parts. He wants us to be honest and transparent — without guile. He wants us to trust Him to meet our needs and not to use cunning devices. This is what Ananias and Sapphira did in New Testament days (see Acts 5:2-4). They misrepresented themselves to the Body of Christ and, in so doing, lied to the Holy Spirit.

Regarding plagiarism, I don't believe that God is referring to the accidental overlooking of referencing our sources, for we all learn from one another and are encouraged by one another. There is very little that is original. Rather, He is concerned with the motives of our hearts. The Lord wants to set us free from the fear that we are not good enough and also from dependence on the praise of others. These things often stem from the pain of rejection and criticism in our early years, and God wants to heal us.

There are many reasons we struggle. Some children

grow up surrounded by chaos: drunken parents screaming abuse, and physical violence or the constant threat of it. The crazy kind of communication that goes on in such households leaves children utterly confused. They don't feel safe, and they feel neglected. The unspoken message they receive is, "There is no one here to protect you; you have to look after yourself."

These children make an effort to control what goes on around them, and they grow up to become controlling adults. Controlling adults began as frightened little children, deprived of the protective structures God planned for families. It's no wonder some of these children grow into angry, rebellious teenagers, who believe they have been let down or "ripped off" by the authority figures in their lives.

The ironic thing about people who were raised in homes of alcoholics is that they have difficulty leaving home. They may move away physically, but they carry emotional baggage with them in the form of various coping behaviors designed to make their bizarre world tolerable. They may develop wonderful social skills, be the life of the party and put people at ease by wisecracking their way through life — anything to avert a disaster. People with such childhood backgrounds may be high achievers and yet not be able to enjoy their own success because of deep, nagging guilt, sadness and loneliness.

Some never get over their sense of loss and simply stay depressed. Some may even sabotage their own success, owing to feelings of worthlessness and mis-directed loyalty. For others, compulsive behavior, in its various forms, may be the legacy of a childhood in a crazy house — anything, including addiction to alcohol or drugs, gambling, eating disorders and sexual deviancy. Explosive, angry outbursts and ag-gression may be the constant companion of many. And the sad thing is that these counterproductive be-haviors are passed on from parents to their children.

The overwhelming sense of powerlessness experi-enced by children in alcoholic homes is often carried into adulthood, with men and women being emo-tionally truncated — still feeling like ten-year-olds inside. This applies to Christians, too — until the Lord heals them. And yet, this potential minefield of a background is often not recognized as a possible cause of failure to progress spiritually.

I remember doing some counseling work with a gentle, caring man, a pastor, who was doing his best to serve God, his congregation, his wife and his fam-ily. This man was trying so hard to please that he had a stress breakdown, and by the time I saw him, he was unable to function in his usual roles. As we ex-plored the reasons for his collapse, it became apparent that the years of repeated abuse and violence from his alcoholic father had left their mark. He could remember returning home often late in the afternoon as a boy, only to find himself locked out of the house, and having to find somewhere to sleep for the night.

At the age of nineteen, this man had found Christ as his Savior, and so the healing work began. But the confusion over his own sense of identity caused his longing for recognition, acceptance and approval to simply be switched from dad to God, and his striving brought on a breakdown.

Not everyone who has been abused rebels; some just try harder to please.

In trying to figure out what it is that blocks our freedom and our progress in the things of God, we can become quite puzzled. I have seen many people come for counseling, completely overwhelmed by their emotions, quite out of control. Most of these people were under the impression that they were having a mental breakdown. The depression was so bad they could not see the light at the end of the tunnel and felt life was not worth living. Tears flowed continually.

In talking to such people, it became apparent to me that many of them had sustained a serious loss, or accumulation of losses, in their recent past and were, in fact, grieving. Because they had not realized that their emotions could become overpowering, they became afraid of what they were feeling, and they were also confused. It was a self-perpetuating cycle.

It would be worthwhile for me to briefly describe

here the grieving process, because we are all touched by it in some way. It is not only when a loved one dies that we grieve. We grieve whenever we sustain a loss of something important to us. If our house burns down, our dog gets run over, we sustain financial loss, job loss, loss of status or even physical disability, we will experience, to varying degrees, the emotions associated with the grieving process. When we realize that hopes, plans or dreams we had for the future will not be realized, we experience loss of expectation, and the disappointment leads to grieving at some level — depending on the importance of the failed ambition to our lives.

I have seen people stuck in the various stages of grieving, and there is usually a good reason they keep going around in circles, finding it difficult to complete the process.

The first reaction we have to loss is to feel shock or perhaps go into denial because the pain is too great to bear. Our mind flicks a switch and shuts off our emotions temporarily, while we attempt to deal with our sense of disorientation. A woman in her seventies came for counseling help many years ago, wondering why she was so weepy and depressed seven months after her husband's death. Her Christian friends had praised her greatly, declaring that her faith in the Lord and sense of peace at this difficult time had been an inspiration to them all. She said she had barely shown any emotion at her husband's funeral, but remained greatly composed.

At the time of his death, staff at the nursing home, where her husband had been cared for, had said it would be better not to view the body. They suggested that she should just get on with her life. Seven months later, she came out of denial and began to feel her emotions, confront her loss and attempt to say good-bye. The well-meaning, but uninformed, advice she was given had hindered the usual progression through the phases of grief.

Another young man, also in the early stages of griev-ing an untimely death (that of his father), turned up in my office absolutely distraught. He was only eigh-teen years old and was desperately trying to be strong, to be the man of the house and to protect his mum and his brother. Under the mistaken belief that the way to be strong was not to talk about the loss, nor cry in front of loved ones, he was bottling everything up and was like a dam about to burst. He cried like a baby for a long time. This emotional release and a little information about what he was going through were enough to move him through the process.

It is important to say here that adults who may have had a parent die or leave when they were little chil-dren have often never sufficiently grieved that loss. They were too young to understand adequately at the time, and throughout life, have continued to experi-

ence a gnawing emptiness and longing, never understanding why. The same experience often occurs in
people who were abandoned or adopted as babies
or young children, regardless of the reason. For
women who felt pressured to give their babies up for
adoption at birth or those who have had abortions,
the grieving may seem never to end.

Some folk find themselves battling guilt feelings
and blaming themselves for what has happened. Still
others complain of constant anger and irritation and
are puzzled by their own behavior. These emotions
are a normal part of grieving, as are feelings of depression, sadness and loss. They seem to have
something to do with feeling out of control and being powerless to alter what has happened. Something
in our lives has changed and will never be the same
again. It takes a big adjustment, and for a while, we
are emotionally disorganized.

Just how big an adjustment life's changes can demand was brought home to me when a young man
in his late twenties came for help because of deep
depression and social withdrawal. This young fellow
said he felt very inadequate socially and found it difficult to make conversation and to meet people,
especially young ladies. As a result, he was very lonely.
As we talked, I could find no reason for any of his
symptoms. He described his family as large and loving, his job as satisfying and his few friends as

supportive. So why was he plummeting into such a serious depression?

The answer came when the young man returned a detailed questionnaire I give my clients to fill in. It became clear to me when I read his answers to questions about his physical health. As a teenager of fourteen, this young man had been diagnosed with juvenile diabetes. This serious disease had devastated his life. He was not given any counseling help at the time of diagnosis, but was left to fend for himself with life and death issues, without anyone understanding the extent of his emotional need for support. He made a decision that this would be his secret. He felt so different from normal teenage boys that he simply buried his secret, told no one except immediate family and attempted to get on with his life. He was never given an opportunity to grieve the loss of his physical health, and because his feelings were suppressed, he had never completed the process of grieving, and thus had never come to closure.

When I pointed out what I believed to be the problem, the young man broke down and wept for the first time in the fifteen years since his diagnosis. He made rapid progress from that point on. The depression lifted, and a greater level of confidence ensued. He became so open that I was able to talk to him about the things of God and subsequently lead him to Christ. This is rather typical. I have found, on many occasions, that if the crises in people's lives are first dealt with, and they are no longer distracted by over-powering emotions, many will respond to the message of salvation.

Possibly one of the most devastating areas of loss in people's lives is due to sexual abuse. When little children are used to meet other people's needs, rather than being protected as they should be, there is a profound loss of trust in relationships that occurs as a result. Not only does it become very difficult for those who have been abused to trust people again, but the shame and the loss of self-respect, innocence and confidence that children and young people experience as a result of being violated in this way is far-reaching and carries ongoing effects into adult life.

Some of the most heart-wrenching stories I've heard recounted over the years have come from homosexuals who desperately did not want to be homosexual, but who were experiencing great anguish confronting some conflicting message from childhood. Men who were sodomized as children in orphanages, men who, as little boys, were dressed as girls until school age because mothers wanted daughters, or lesbians, whose dads wanted sons, deserve the same compassion and unconditional love from us that God gives them. This is not approving their sin; it is reaching out to their need.

I do not think I can stress enough the importance

of learning to confront emotionally painful issues as they occur and to deal with them as quickly as possible. If we do not do this, our pain tends to be buried, and we experience inner turmoil and fear. We put up all kinds of walls to protect ourselves, and we tend to develop comfort behaviors. We look for ways to fill our inner emptiness. Alcohol, cigarettes, drugs, gambling, sex, food, shopping, television, sports, pornography ... anything that temporarily distracts us and momentarily relieves the pain will do. Such false comforts might briefly bolster our flagging self-esteem and block the fear, but the truth is, this substitution is basically idolatry and is, therefore, bound to fail. Anything we look to in place of God will ultimately let us down. When something is not the real thing, it cannot give us true inner peace. Only our heavenly Father can do that.

To be in emotional bondage usually means we are also in spiritual bondage. When we experience suffering at the hands of other individuals, we are usually unaware that we are holding unforgiveness and, perhaps, are guilty of judging the people who have hurt us. In looking at the facts regarding the reality of our situations, we are not blaming our parents or others around us, for they, too, have been wounded before us. Judgment is the task of God alone, and if we judge, we find that we hold ourselves captive spiritually — without even knowing it. Then, we wonder why we are not experiencing the liberty that is ours through Christ.

God has not left us without answers to our human dilemmas. Rather, the power of the cross is so great and so complete that we can have utter confidence in a God who has done all that is necessary to set us free and completely heal us. But in order to receive the promises of God and walk in liberty, we need to have a good grasp of what God has done for us in sending His Son. We need to understand the power of the finished work on the cross — the power of the blood of Jesus. We need to comprehend the totality of the victory of Christ over our sins, our sicknesses and our sorrows.

For in Christ there is all of God in a human body; so you have everything when you have Christ, and you are filled with God through your union with Christ. He is the highest Ruler, with authority over every other power.

When you came to Christ he set you free from your evil desires, not by a bodily operation of circumcision but by a spiritual operation, the baptism of your souls.

You were dead in sins, and your sinful desires were not yet cut away. Then he gave you a share in the very life of Christ, for he forgave all your sins, and blotted out the charges proved against you, the list of his commandments which you had not obeyed. He took this list of sins and destroyed it by nailing it to Christ's cross. In this way God took away Satan's power to accuse you of sin, and God openly displayed to the whole world Christ's triumph at the cross where your sins were all taken away.

Colossians 2:9-11 and 13-15, TLB

Three

&

God's Solution

to the Human Struggle

*Y*ou may be wondering what struggle I am referring to. Recently, I saw a slogan on a T-shirt which probably sums up what life is like for untold millions of people. Someone was honest enough to own up to how bad he was feeling. Slapped across this young man's chest were the words: "Life sucks, and then you die."

Our human condition and the oppressive features of society have been pondered by philosophers for centuries. Where did we come from? Where are we going? What is the meaning of life? And what is the nature of the human struggle?

There is yet another question constantly asked relating to the quality of human life. Aristotle called this the "human good" and wondered how to attain it. In the literature regarding human beings and the source of our troubles — whether it be philosophical, psychological, theological or sociological — there appears to be general agreement about one point: there is such a thing as "the good life," and human beings struggle to attain it.

While there is diversity of opinion regarding what "the good life" entails and what it would look like if it could be attained, there is continual reference to our condition of alienation, or estrangement, from our true selves and our original source. In other words, we do not understand our true condition; we have lost our way and, hence, live unsatisfying, frustrated lives.

A debate about this topic raged in the nineteenth century and spilled over into the twentieth century in such developments as existentialism and "critical social theory." Philosophers like Hegel, Marx and Nietzsche were among the leading contributors to the debate, and their ideas have been much discussed.

Brian Fay, in his book *Critical Social Science*, discusses the theory of self-estrangement, or existential alienation, in some detail. He uses the parable of the cave in Plato's *Republic* to highlight what he is saying. According to the allegory:

"Down in the bowels of a cave, chained in such a way that they can only see the shadows of objects projected onto the wall in front of them, ordinary human beings live in a world of illusion, which, in their ignorance, they take to be real. Their collective existence is structured on this mistaken belief, so that they organize themselves around pointless, misconceived activities. However, one of them escapes from the cave, sees the falseness of his or her life, and eventually comes to look directly at the sun, which is the source of all light." [1] Plato's metaphor depicts life as an illusion, with individuals being ignorant of their own ignorance of reality.

This is the frightening truth for all those who do not know Christ as their Savior. It was the truth for the young man with the depressing slogan across his chest, and it should stir us to compassion — compassion for the lost.

The truth about reality is revealed to us in Jesus Christ, and His death for our sins exposes the nature of the human struggle. Philosophers throughout the ages have wondered why life is such an uphill battle and have wondered what could be done to improve our lot.

They were right about one thing — the human race is separated from its original Creator. What they failed to understand was the reason — sin. The nature of the human struggle is not economic, as Marx stated, nor meaninglessness, as Sartre stated, nor is it ignorance as others have claimed. It is sin. Revolution is not the answer, and neither is suicide. The real problem is sin, and Jesus Christ is the answer to sin.

This life is not a dress rehearsal for the real thing. This *is* the real thing! We have only one opportunity to come to an understanding of reality as God made it and to adjust to the way things really are, not the way we would like them to be. For that reason, it is important for us to grasp God's overall plan for humanity, to understand and apprehend what God has done for us. What He offers us through Jesus Christ is the most empowering experience we can have. Salvation sets us free and gives us the abundant life, and that's what all those philosophers were trying to find. Freedom through Christ is indeed the "good life," and it is available to us through the new covenant God made with the human race through His Son, Jesus Christ.

In order to understand fully our inheritance in Christ and to benefit from the new covenant blessings, it is necessary to discuss in some detail how God's plan for humanity works. We tend to understand this piecemeal, as we listen to sermons, read books and study chapters of the Bible one at a time. But if we can develop an overview, it is more powerful in its impact. At least, then, we understand clearly what it is we are reaching out for.

I remember how the president of the Bible college I attended described his time on the mission field to the students. As a missionary in South America, he experienced, for the first time, the powerful clash between the powers of darkness and the power of God. When he saw people delivered from demonic bondage and saw the awesome power of the finished work of the cross setting people free, he really became a "believer." Head knowledge suddenly became revelation knowledge.

Those memories returned for me recently after a mission trip to Africa, where I saw and experienced firsthand the great need of the people. I also saw the clash of the powers of darkness with the Kingdom of Light, as people came and asked for prayer to break curses off their lives. Many Christians shared about their struggles with family members who were involved in witchcraft, with cultural expectations opposing a Christian lifestyle, and with lack of understanding of God's Word in general. They simply did not know how to combat their difficult circumstances.

When I returned home, I began to realize more deeply the great need in the Body of Christ for foundational teaching regarding the power of the blood of Jesus. As we study the blood of Jesus, we gain a deeper comprehension of God's promises. A passage, familiar to us all, talks about this:

> *While they were eating, Jesus took bread, gave thanks and broke it, and gave it to his disciples,*

saying "Take and eat; this is my body." Then he
took the cup, gave thanks and offered it to them,
saying, "Drink from it, all of you. This is my
blood of the covenant, which is poured out for
many for the forgiveness of sins."

Matthew 26:26-28

We often read this passage of scripture when we take communion. Here, Jesus is talking about His blood of the covenant, and each time we take communion we are confessing our loyalty to Christ and to the Church. In doing this, we are ratifying or reinforcing the blood covenant God has made with us through Jesus Christ.

The word *covenant* means "a solemn oath or vow which can never be broken." In the Hebrew, the word for covenant means "to cut" and has the suggestion of an incision from which blood flows. [2] A covenant is not like a contract we use today in which, if one party fails to keep the agreement, it can be broken. A covenant is a unilateral agreement, a promise that is made and must be kept.

The reason it is so important for us, as Christians, to understand this is that God operates with us on the basis of covenant. This is the way He relates to us. So, if we want to relate to God, we need to understand covenant. We, in the Western world, are not familiar with covenants, and therefore we fail to understand the power available to us through our covenant with God. We often do not use what is ours because we do not know we have it.

In this way, we become strangers through our failure to access what is rightfully ours. It's a bit like having insurance and then not making a claim on it when we have a need, simply because we have not read the fine print to see what was included.

Unlike in the West, in many parts of the world today, people still practice blood covenant rites similar to the Lord's table, just as ancient civilizations have done for centuries.

Covenants are usually made for one of three reasons: protection, business or out of the bond of love. In fact, history shows that in the primitive mind there has always been a belief that inter-communion with God could be possible through inter-union by blood. Since God is life, blood is life and all life belongs to God, the belief is that blood is a means of inter-union with Him. Shedding the blood of a sacrificial offering to God has, for centuries, been considered an act of gratitude to God and a way of partaking of His strengths — that is, becoming like him. [3]

This was, no doubt, how cannibalism came about. In humanity's search for oneness with God or other gods, there was a perverted belief that drinking the blood and eating the flesh of a consecrated human being would achieve a sharing of the divine nature and attributes.

The missionary journeys of Dr. David Livingstone contain stories concerning blood covenants. Both he and Henry Stanley, the journalist who went to search for Livingstone in Africa, found it necessary to "cut covenant" with local people on several occasions.

A blood covenant was never entered into lightly. Before the actual ceremony could take place, several things had to happen. In a typical ceremony, the rights and obligations of the agreement were discussed first, in order to ensure that both parties were able to fulfill their vows. Next, they exchanged gifts, and only their best, most treasured possessions were given. The next step was the actual cutting and exchanging of blood. This was done either by dripping the blood into a glass of wine and drinking it or by cutting wrists and rubbing them together.

Afterwards, gunpowder was rubbed into the wound as a permanent mark of this special relationship. Then, a tree was planted as a memorial, or a pile of stones was erected in honor of two men becoming blood brothers. [4]

Although the methods used in covenant ceremonies varied from place to place, the intention remained the same.

It is important to understand that when two men became blood brothers, the strength of one party became the strength of the other party. Covenant meant that you shared everything with your blood brother. You protected one another and met one another's needs. This sacred bond was treated with great honor and, according to Livingstone and Stanley, it was not known to have ever been broken. Terrible curses were pronounced over anyone who dared to break the bond of covenant friendship.

Stanley ran into trouble with some local tribes in Africa while he was searching for Dr. Livingstone. He had difficulty with a powerful, very warlike, equatorial tribe which would not allow him and his men safe passage through their territory. After initial conflict with the chief, and at the suggestion of his interpreter, Stanley decided to approach the man seeking blood-covenant friendship, so they could become allies and no longer be enemies. As much as Stanley was repulsed by the idea, he did it out of necessity. The old chief agreed, after an initial discussion regarding motives and ability to keep the covenant.

In this particular case, substitutes were used for the two men in the ceremony. An African prince represented the chief, while one of Stanley's men from England took his place. This use of substitutes was not an uncommon practice.

Stanley found the exchanging of gifts difficult in this agreement, because the old chief asked for his prized goat. Stanley was in a state of ill health and needed the goat's milk for his sick stomach. He reluctantly agreed, however, and in exchange, was given the chief's seven-foot-long spear. He was convinced this was an uneven exchange and wondered what he would do with a useless spear.

Much to his surprise and delight, Stanley found, as he traveled with the chief's spear, that it carried great power. Upon recognizing it, the local people submitted to Stanley, wherever he went, and allowed him to safely pass through their territory. [5]

God is an initiator of covenants. In fact, the Bible is full of covenants. God made covenants with Adam, Noah, Abraham, Moses and David. Each time God made a new covenant, He related to humanity on different terms, so ushering in new dispensations. These covenants were part of the progressive revelation of God and were designed to bring about the plan and purpose of God for us. [6]

God's covenant with Abraham is of particular interest. Inasmuch as there is interrelatedness between all of the covenants, it was through Abraham that God prophesied the chosen nation of Israel, through which the Messiah would come, and all the earth would be blessed through the messianic seed.

The Abrahamic covenant was the most comprehensive of all the Old Testament covenants, and it was made not only with Abraham, but was also renewed with Isaac and confirmed to Jacob (Israel) after him (see 1 Chronicles 16:15-17).

When God entered into covenant fellowship with Abraham, He promised several things: that He would be as a shield and reward (see Genesis 15:1), that Abraham would have many descendants (see Genesis 15:5) and that the land of Canaan would be Abraham's inheritance (see Genesis 15:7). Abraham's part in this was to accept, in faith, God's promises and walk in obedience before Him.

When God cut the covenant with Abraham, He told him to bring a heifer, a goat, a ram, a dove and a pigeon. Then Abraham cut each of the sacrifices in two and laid the two halves opposite each other. The Scriptures go on to say:

> *When the sun had set and darkness had fallen, a smoking firepot with a blazing torch appeared and passed between the pieces. On that day the* Lord *made a covenant with Abram and said, "To your descendants I give this land."*
>
> Genesis 15:17-18

The custom of the day was to slaughter the animals, cut them in half, place the halves opposite each other and then have the parties to the agreement walk between them. This act was symbolic of what would happen to them if they failed to keep the covenant. They would perish just like the slain animals.

In this scriptural passage, the *"smoking firepot with*

a blazing torch" represented God's presence. Usually, in a covenant agreement, there were responsibilities for both parties. In this case, however, only God passed between the animals, because it was He alone who established the promises and obligations of the covenant.

God's covenant with Abraham was sealed with circumcision (see Genesis 17:9-12), and God told Abraham that he and his descendants must obey the covenant for generations to come and that He would bless them as a result. When each male child was circumcised on the eighth day after birth, he entered into the covenant and became an heir of everything connected with it.

The covenant bound Abraham and his descendants by indissoluble ties to God, and it bound God to Abraham and the nation of Israel. As long as the people of Israel kept the covenant, they would have God's protection and provision.

God greatly tested Abraham's faith by calling him to leave his land and his people and travel to an unknown destination. After Abraham had waited twenty-five years for the fulfillment of the promise of an heir, God asked him to sacrifice his much-beloved son Isaac (see Genesis 22:2). When God saw that Abraham was willing to obey and keep the covenant agreement", to be obedient and blameless before Him, He continued the blessings. Just as God tested

Abraham's faith, so He will test us, to see if our hope is in Him or in something else.

I pointed out earlier that the ancient practice of blood covenants developed out of the belief that the life is in the blood. Therefore, blood is the most precious of commodities. In our modern Western society, we tend to view spilled blood as representing death and find it abhorrent. This is not so in many other cultures. In fact, in ancient times, when a king was establishing a new kingdom, he would travel from village to village in order to explain the rules of his kingdom to the people. Those subjects who were loyal to the king would put blood on the doorposts at the entrance to their houses, as a sign of welcome and honor to the king. If no blood was seen around the entrance when the king passed by, he sent in his soldiers to kill the disloyal subjects. [7]

It is this tradition of the threshold covenant which gives us greater understanding of what occurred at Passover. In Exodus 12, we read that God told Moses to instruct the Israelites to kill a lamb for each household and put its blood on the sides and top of the doorframes of the houses. According to the ancient tradition, with which the people were already familiar, this was to be a sign of welcome, an invitation for the king to enter. God was the King who was passing by that night.

There are two Hebrew words for the term *pass by* —

abar and *pesah*. *Abar* was used in the story of Moses, when he was hidden in the cleft of the rock and God passed by (see Exodus 33:22). *Pesah* means "to leap over or cross a threshold," and it is this word that was used in Exodus 12:23 to indicate that God's presence entered in over the threshold of the entrance of those houses that had blood on the doorposts. [8] The presence of God protected the Israelites from the angel of death, who struck down the firstborn of the Egyptians. Thus, the verse reads like this:

> *When the LORD goes through* [abar] *the land to strike down the Egyptians, he will see the blood on the top and sides of the doorframe and will pass over* [pesah] *that doorway, and he will not permit the destroyer to enter your houses and strike you down.*   Exodus 12:23

In the Middle East, this tradition is still practiced today. Blood is placed at the doorway to welcome and honor guests, and the importance of the guests is indicated by the size of the animal sacrificed to produce the blood. Small animals, like pigeons, may be used for people of lesser importance, while the "fatted calf" is kept for a king or someone considered to be of equal importance.

The owner of the home promises, according to this custom, to protect the guest with his very life. This practice is taken very seriously, and the utmost duty of care is exercised in making sure guests feel at home and all their needs are met. The story of Lot, when the two angels visited him in Sodom (see Genesis 19), highlights this ancient tradition. The homosexuals of the city clamored around the front door, wanting the visitors to come out, so they could have sex with them. Lot refused, saying, *"Don't do anything to these men, for they have come under the protection of my roof"* (Genesis 19:8), and he offered his virgin daughters instead. It is difficult to believe that any father could do such a thing, but this passage reveals the strength of the blood covenant, the promise of full protection to anyone who entered in over the threshold. [9]

It was considered a great insult to step in the blood at the doorway. The expectation was that the guests would see the blood, understand the welcome and step over the blood in respect for the host. After all, the host was willing to protect the guest with his life. The writer of Hebrews, then, showed how serious this offense was:

> *How much more severely do you think a man deserves to be punished who has trampled the Son of God under foot, who has treated as an unholy thing the blood of the covenant that sanctified him, and who has insulted the Spirit of grace?*   Hebrew 10:29

This passage clearly refers to the practice of placing blood at the doorway of the home, and speaks of the great insult it represents if the sacrificial blood of Jesus is rejected. As Christians, if we keep on sinning after coming to a knowledge of the truth, this is equivalent to stepping on or standing in the blood at the doorway.

Christ instituted a new covenant when He died for us. The blood of Jesus represents the blood around the doorpost, just as the blood at Passover foreshadowed the coming Savior, the Messiah, and His sacrifice for us. As Christians, we have accepted the invitation to step across into covenant relationship with God, the Master of the house, and receive the protection and blessings that flow from Him. God has given to Abraham's seed His most treasured possession, the best gift possible, His one and only Son, as His covenant gift.

In exchange, we give ourselves, our lives, our wills, so that we are wholly His, and He is wholly ours. Everything God is and has now belongs to us through Christ. Because we are in covenant relationship, however, we lose all rights to ourselves. We are to be totally at God's disposal, as He sees fit.

The reason we can become so excited about the new covenant instituted by Christ is that Jesus died for our sins, our sicknesses and our sorrows (see Isaiah 53:4-5). Every need we could possibly ever have in life is met in Jesus Christ. When we have Him, we have everything. This is why it is not necessary to do anything to try to add to the finished work of the cross. The blood of chickens and goats no longer need be shed to secure favor from God. There are no lucky charms or superstitious acts that can enhance the power of the cross.

The human struggle to cope with meaninglessness and the fear of death has been conquered. Anyone who desires to know God personally and experience the liberty of living in Him daily can do so simply by repenting and believing upon Jesus Christ as his or her personal Lord and Savior (see Mark 1:15).

The new covenant Christ purchased for us is better than the old because the new covenant cleanses and completely removes sin, as though it never happened, while the old covenant only covered sin. The blood of Jesus cleanses our consciences so that we can stand before God without condemnation. The blood of animals only cleansed the flesh.

In times past, God dwelt in the Holy of Holies in the Temple, but now He dwells in our bodies through the Holy Spirit. At Christ's death, the curtain in the Temple was torn in two, which meant the end of blood on the Mercy Seat. Now, we could legally be taken from Satan's authority and restored to fellowship with God.

With an understanding of the all-sufficient power

of the blood of Jesus, which grants us total access to the Father, Psalm 91 takes on new meaning:

> *He who dwells in the shelter of the Most High will rest in the shadow of the Almighty. I will say of the LORD, "He is my refuge and my fortress, my God, in whom I trust."* Psalm 91:1

This psalm is talking about coming under the protection of the roof of the Almighty God of Heaven and earth. The psalmist refers to the complete safety of entering into covenant relationship with Him. The blood of Jesus has been sprinkled around the doorframes, and we are invited to step across as honored guests, as kings and queens, so to speak, to partake of all that Christ is and has — to know God as a safe refuge, a fortress against the enemy. As we dwell in covenant relationship with God, our very lives are protected by the Master of the house.

Christ's victory over sin and death is total and complete. Satan can only take what we give him. Just as Stanley discovered that the chief's spear carried total authority, and the enemy tribes bowed to him when they saw the spear he carried, so the powers of darkness must bow to us when we come covered by the blood of Jesus. The chief's spear was the peace offering Stanley needed in Africa, in order to dwell in safety. The shedding of Christ's blood is the peace offering we need to secure a safe passage through life and on into eternity.

When God was about to flood the earth because of its wickedness, He told Noah to build the ark as protection, as a safe passage through the flood. Jesus is now our ark, through the new covenant. The name of Jesus is all-powerful, and when we belong to Him, we can use His name. The depth of this truth was brought home to me early one morning several years ago, when I was awakened from sleep by something which felt extremely heavy, somewhat like a slab of concrete on top of me. As I roused myself to consciousness, I became aware of the fact that I was paralyzed by this oppressive presence upon my physical body. I could not utter a sound; all the muscles in my body were frozen. I could not even cry out.

In my shock and panic, I did the only thing I could do — I *thought* the name "Jesus," and when I did this, the demonic force lifted off me instantly. That day I learned the truth of the promise:

> *We are more than conquerors through him who loved us. For I am convinced that neither death nor life, neither angels nor demons, neither the present nor the future, nor any powers, neither height nor depth, not anything else in all creation, will be able to separate us from the love of God that is in Christ Jesus our Lord.*
>
> Romans 8:37-39

O God, you are my God, earnestly I seek you; my soul thirsts for you, my body longs for you, in a dry and weary land where there is no water.

I have seen you in the sanctuary and beheld your power and your glory.

Because your love is better than life, my lips will glorify you.

I will praise you as long as I live, and in your name I will lift up my hands.

My soul will be satisfied as with the richest of food; with singing lips my mouth will praise you.

On my bed I remember you; I think of you through the watches of the night.

Because you are my help, I sing in the shadow of your wings.

My soul clings to you; your right hand upholds me. Psalm 63:1-8

Four

❦

In Step With the Spirit

One morning, about eighteen months ago, I was in my room praying, when suddenly my eyes were opened to see in the Spirit, and I found myself watching a picture. This picture was like a movie, and it had four parts to it.

First, I saw myself as a musical instrument, and the Holy Spirit was playing beautiful music upon my life, as I surrendered to Him. This music was wafting like incense up to the throne of God.

Then, suddenly, the picture widened, and I saw all the other Christians who were also surrendering to the Holy Spirit. They, too, were being played as instruments, and beautiful music was rising from their lives like incense — a *Sweet Aroma* to God.

Then the picture changed. I found myself looking at a large orchestra, and all the instruments were being tuned and made ready to play a symphony. I was aware of some discordant sounds, but the various instruments were being prepared to make just the right sound, so they could all harmonize together.

I could see the back of the Conductor standing there, waiting for the right moment to begin. I knew the Conductor was the Holy Spirit, and I sensed that the symphony, which was about to begin, was extremely important. I understood the symphony to be the end-time move of God in bringing in the last harvest of souls before Christ returns.

It was a solemn moment. Suddenly, the Conductor raised His hand and pointed to several people who were tuning their instruments. He told them they had to leave; they were not allowed to play in the symphony because their instruments were out of tune. Time had run out; the symphony was about to begin, and they were not ready. They were, therefore, unable to take their places.

As I watched these people leave the stage, the Spirit of God descended upon me with what I can only describe as grief-stricken anguish. Suddenly, I was getting a glimpse of the pain and distress in the heart of God over those in the Church who are excluding themselves because they are not following the voice of the Holy Spirit. They are preoccupied with earthly things and are not listening; they are not keeping in step with the Holy Spirit. I found myself in a heap on the floor, sobbing and wailing, as the heart of God surged through me momentarily.

When the Spirit lifted, the atmosphere was very solemn. I was aware of the seriousness of what had been revealed to me. I had also glimpsed God's amazing love for us, His desire that all should participate in this final thrust of His love in the earth. This all had to do with the Great Commission. Jesus said:

> *"All authority in heaven and on earth has been given to me. Therefore go and make disciples of all nations, baptizing them in the name of the Father and of the Son and of the Holy Spirit, and teaching them to obey everything I have commanded you. And surely I am with you always, to the very end of the age."*
>
> Matthew 28:18-20

God's people are told to go and preach the Gospel in all the world. But first, Jesus said, we must wait for the promise of the Father, which is the power of the Holy Spirit that will enable us to get the job done. We cannot do it without the Holy Spirit.

Jesus told His disciples:

> *"Do not leave Jerusalem, but wait for the gift my Father promised, which you have heard me speak about. For John baptized with water, but*

in a few days you will be baptized with the Holy Spirit.

"You will receive power when the Holy Spirit comes on you; and you will be my witnesses in Jerusalem, and in all Judea and Samaria, and to the ends of the earth."   Acts 1:4-5 and 8

Before we can be witnesses, we need to be disciples, and we need to be disciples before we can make other disciples. A disciple knows the ways of the one he or she is following. It is the Holy Spirit who teaches us the ways of Jesus. This is why it is so important to know how to hear the voice of the Holy Spirit and to follow Him. The Holy Spirit will never say anything contrary to the Word of God, so it is important to become familiar with biblical teaching.

If we keep in step with the Spirit (see Galatians 5:25), then we will live by His power and so not gratify the desires of the sinful nature, for they are in conflict with God's Spirit (see Galatians 5:16-17).

This phrase, "to keep in step or walk by the Spirit" comes from the Greek word *stoicheo*, which means "to keep a straight line or have right conduct." [1] This means we must come to God in holiness and purity if we want His Spirit to guide our lives, because the flesh and the Spirit are enemies of each other. Sin hinders the Holy Spirit in our lives, and if we want to progress in the things of God, we must get rid of it.

Like the musicians in the orchestra, we are to keep our eyes on the Conductor, anticipating His next move, so we can be ready to move with Him. Paul taught, *"For as many as are led by the Spirit of God, they are the sons of God"* (Romans 8:14, KJV). The Christian life is lived in the power of the Holy Spirit, and without the Holy Spirit, there is no Christian life. All our sentimental actions and kind deeds, if done out of our own heart of flesh, amount to nothing. Anything we do apart from God's Spirit will be burned up. If that's all we have to show, we will have wasted our time here on earth.

If we cultivate the habit of listening carefully to the voice of the Holy Spirit and doing only what He tells us to do, then God will be able to trust us, and He will teach us how to take our places in the Body and fulfill our callings. In this way, our lives will be like beautiful music, like incense, a *Sweet Aroma* ascending to the throne of God. Our lives will be fragrant to the extent to which the Holy Spirit flows out of us. The Lord tells us:

> *"I will require your offerings and the firstfruits of your sacrifices, together with all your holy things. I will accept you as a SWEET AROMA."*
> Ezekiel 20:40-41, NKJ

If Jesus wants us to be His faithful disciples and

powerful witnesses to fulfil the Great Commission, how do we go about doing that? God has given us a pattern to follow. Long before Christ came as Savior to the earth, God foreshadowed His ministry and high priestly calling in the pattern of the Tabernacle of Moses.

Throughout the Bible, God's love for humanity is revealed in His thoughtful and detailed planning to secure our redemption. God always had a plan to live among His people. He told Moses, *"Have them make a sanctuary for me, and I will dwell among them"* (Exodus 25:8). The Tabernacle, a tent that Moses set up according to God's detailed instructions, was the place where the Lord chose to dwell among and meet with His people during that time. The cloud of God's glory rested over the Tabernacle day and night, and whenever the cloud lifted from above the tent, the people would set off for some other spot. This was God's way of guiding the Israelites during the time they wandered in the wilderness for forty years.

There were actually four temporary dwellings of the Lord recorded in the Scriptures: Noah's ark, the Tabernacle of Moses, the Tabernacle of David and the Temple of Solomon. [2] These temporary abodes were symbolic, illustrating the story of redemption, a picture of what Christ was going to do for us, a pattern of living desired of us by God. We can learn much about the Christian life by studying the Tabernacle and its furniture, for it was merely a shadow of the reality that was to come.

As we look at the physical composition of this Old Testament meeting place, we can see how it pointed toward the time when we, the believers in Jesus Christ, would be the spiritual tabernacle of God. Even the shape of the Israelites' camp was symbolic. The twelve tribes set up camp in the shape of a cross, with the Tabernacle in the center. The Levites camped closest to the entrance, since they were the priests who ministered to the people.

The Tabernacle had an Outer Court and an Inner Court. The Inner Court consisted of the Holy Place and the Holy of Holies where the Ark of the Covenant was kept. The first, and largest, piece of equipment, or furniture, in the Outer Court was the Brazen Altar, where the animal sacrifices for sin took place. This slaughter place was the approach to God, and it speaks to us of Christ's death on the cross for our sins. It also speaks of our death to self, as we identify with Christ and learn dependence upon God. The altar was made of wood, which speaks of Christ's humanity, and it was overlaid with brass, which speaks of judgment and endurance.

After killing the sacrificial animal, whose blood was shed to cover the sins of the Israelites, the priest would proceed to the Laver, which was a bowl with water used to wash his hands and feet before proceeding into the Tabernacle itself. The bronze Laver represents the Word of God. It speaks to us of separating from the world through confession of sin — a yielding of ourselves to God for His service alone. [3] The Laver is a picture of the sanctifying, purifying, cleansing power of God's Word, which qualifies us for ministry by washing away defilement and granting access to God's holiness. We need to be washed continually.

The priest would then move to the Holy Place, which had no natural light, only the light that came from the Golden Lampstand, a seven-branched candlestick. The Golden Lampstand was filled with pure olive oil and was to burn continually and, thus, represent the ministry of the Holy Spirit in our lives, giving revelation and illumination. The Lampstand represents both the Lord Jesus Christ and the written Word of God. The gold speaks of His deity, the oil and fire represent the Holy Spirit, and the wicks represent us, the believer priests, who are submerged (literally, baptized) in the Holy Spirit (oil) and set ablaze by His fire. Twice a day, the priest would trim the wicks so the lamp would burn brightly. We, too, will be pruned so that we more brightly reflect God's glory.

We are to walk only by the light of the Word of God. Natural light is the light of human reason. Following human reason leads to the rejection of God's Word and the development of human philosophies and natural wisdom. [4]

The lamps on the Lampstand shed light on the Table of Shewbread, where twelve loaves of bread were placed daily. The priests ate the bread, fellowshipped with each other and communed with God around this table. We commune with God as we partake of the Bread of Life, Jesus Christ (see John 6:35). Frankincense was poured on the bread before it was eaten, and this speaks of the Holy Spirit and the manner in which He gives us a desire for the Word of God. The table was made of acacia wood, which speaks of Christ's humanity. Its gold covering speaks of His deity.

There was a third piece of furniture in the Holy Place, the Altar of Incense, which was in the very heart of the Tabernacle and closest to the Veil separating the Holy Place from the Holy of Holies, where God's presence dwelt. This altar was three feet high, the tallest piece of furniture in the Holy Place, and this speaks of the highest act of worship possible, that of prayer and priestly intercession. While the Brazen Altar speaks of the death of Christ, the Golden Altar speaks of the living, resurrected, ascended Christ. The two altars speak of Christ's death and resurrection, and thereby constitute the full message of the Gospel. [5]

When the high priest trimmed the lamps, morning and night, he would also burn fragrant incense on the altar. This is a picture of intercession and worship. The Altar of Incense not only speaks of the worship and intercession of the saints, but also of our great High Priest, Jesus, who intercedes for us at the throne of God. When we, the believer priests, have washed at the Laver and fed on the Shewbread, we can, in the light of the Lampstand, bring true worship to the Lord.

Daily, we need to spend time with the Lord in prayer, for prayer is the foundation of any work the Lord gives us to do. Without prayer, nothing will succeed in the Christian life.

Beyond the Veil was the Holy of Holies, where the Shekinah glory of God resided. The Ark of the Covenant rested there, and once a year, the high priest would enter the Holy of Holies to sprinkle blood on the Mercy Seat to cleanse the people.

There are three arks described in the Bible: the ark of Noah, the ark of Moses and the Ark of the Covenant, which speaks of the ultimate security of the believer from judgment. Noah and his family were kept safe from God's judgment, which came by way of the flood, and Moses was kept safe, as a baby, when Pharaoh decreed that all the male infants should be drowned in the Nile River. Both of these arks were sealed with pitch to keep them watertight. The Hebrew word translated "pitch" in the Bible is *kaphar*, which means "atonement." [6] Both these arks were preparation for the third ark, the Ark of the Covenant, with its bloodstained Mercy Seat above it. Salvation depends on the blood of atonement of an innocent sacrifice.

Jesus Christ is now our Ark, and His blood has obtained mercy for us, once for all:

> *Therefore, brothers, since we have confidence to enter the Most Holy Place by the blood of Jesus, by a new and living way opened for us through the curtain, that is, his body, and since we have a great priest over the house of God, let us draw near to God with a sincere heart in full assurance of faith, having our hearts sprinkled to cleanse us from a guilty conscience and having our bodies washed with pure water.*
>
> Hebrews 10:19-22

It is no longer necessary for the high priest to sprinkle blood on the Mercy Seat. We can freely come into God's presence, because we are sanctified through the offering of the body of Jesus Christ, once and for all. The Veil has been torn in two, signifying permanent and free access to the presence of God. He has made full provision for all our needs.

The power that Jesus promised came on the Day of Pentecost, ten days after His ascension, when all the disciples were gathered together. *"All of them were filled with the Holy Spirit and began to speak in other tongues"* (Acts 2:4). No longer was God dwelling in tabernacles made by human hands, but now we, the Christian believers, became the resting place for God's Holy Spirit: *"For we are the temple of the living God"* (2 Corinthians 6:16).

I have discovered over the years, as I have counseled with Christians, that a large percentage do not understand the Holy Spirit. Beyond knowing that they received the Spirit to dwell within at conversion, they seem to lack the kind of teaching needed to help them go on with the Lord. It is not my intention, in this chapter, to give detailed instruction on how to receive the baptism of the Holy Spirit and minister in the gifts, but it is important for all Christians to know that it is God's desire for us to receive the same powerful anointing that came upon Jesus and His disciples, enabling them to proclaim God's Word with signs and wonders following (see Act 2:43).

While it is the Holy Spirit who gives us power, there is so much more that He is responsible for in God's redemptive purposes. He indwells us and sanctifies us, delivers us from the bondage of sin and motivates us to holy living. The Spirit gives us assurance of salvation, helps us pray and worship, produces Christlike character and guides us into all truth. But more than that, the Holy Spirit was sent by the Father to bring believers into the intimate presence and fellowship of Jesus (see John 14:16-18), to continually pour out God's love into our hearts (see Romans 5:5). [7]

How we long to experience God's love! How we hunger for His intimate presence! How can we achieve it? It is not about know-how or methods. There is no formula for dwelling in God's presence. It's all about heart attitudes. Oswald Chambers says of this:

> *No-one can tell you where the shadow of the Almighty is, you must find that out for you. When you have found out where it is, stay there; under that shadow no evil can ever befall you. The intensity of the moments spent under the shadow of the Almighty is the full measure of your usefulness as a worker. Intensity of communion is not in feelings or emotions or in special places, but in quiet, fixed, confident centering on God. Never allow anything to hinder you from being in the place where your spiritual life is maintained.* [8]

God is concerned with relationship. This is His consuming desire. This is what motivates His heart (see John 3:16). We are so used to earthly fathers teaching us the importance of accomplishment that we think the way to please our heavenly Father also is to do clever things, to achieve. Nothing could be further from the truth. Being clever or not being clever does not affect God's love for us. We do not have to earn His acceptance. He loves us and accepts us un-conditionally, simply because we are made in His image and because it is in His nature to love.

Seeking God is all about yielding to the Holy Spirit. The Bridegroom is wooing the Bride. The Scriptures reveal that everything God has ever done and ever will do, right up to the Marriage Supper of the Lamb, is concerned with only one thing — the gathering out and training of His Bride for her exalted position of co-rulership with her Bridegroom over His eternal Kingdom. The Messiah came with one intent — to give birth to the Church and, thus, obtain His Bride. [9] Communing with God is about responding to the call of the Spirit within, hearing His voice, that still, small voice, as *"deep calls to deep"* (Psalm 42:7).

All we have to do is make a move toward the Lord, just simply respond, and then He will draw even closer to us. It's a dance of intimacy. The Bible tells us that God is a rewarder of those who earnestly seek Him (see Hebrews 11:6). He rewards us with His presence.

Have you ever noticed that when two people fall in love, all they want to do is be together? All day long, they think about each other, anticipating the time when they will be in each other's company. When they do get together, they want to be as close as possible, to touch each other and gaze into one another's eyes. They want to please each other. Two people in love are obsessed. They get rid of all hindrances and distractions so that nothing and no one can come between them — so prized is their relationship. *"I found the one my heart loves. I held him and would not let him go"* (Song of Solomon 3:4).

Whatever we pay attention to in life tends to influence us; we become just like the thing we behold. Martin Luther said, "Whatever your heart clings to and confides in, that is really your God."[10] Jesus said, *"For where your treasure is, there your heart will be also"* (Matthew 6:21). If we really long for a deeper walk with God, if we want to know the reality of living in the peace and joy of the Lord, enjoying the abundant life He promised, then it's all about choices. What are our priorities?

Walking in the power of the Spirit is a progressive thing, and as we learn one step, the Lord takes us to the next step. He keeps everything simple. If our desire is to surrender to the Holy Spirit, then He will teach us how. Jesus said, *"If anyone chooses to do God's will, he will find out whether my teaching comes from God or whether I speak on my own"* (John 7:17). Revelation comes as we make a sincere commitment to obey. God withholds understanding from those who are only playing games. It's all about attitude, not cleverness.

I can remember, as a new Christian, how I lacked understanding of the ways of the Lord. I had a strong

desire to follow the Holy Spirit, but my prayers were
way off base because I had little Bible knowledge. I
remember praying earnestly that God would make
me like the wise Christians I looked up to in the
Church. I did not realize that I was asking for instant
maturity. I believed God could do anything, but I
hadn't learned yet about the things He would not do.
I so much wanted to have the knowledge these other
people had and be able to do what I saw them do. I
am embarrassed now, as I look back at my own ignorance of God's ways, but He spoke to me very
gently, and I came to understand about progressive
revelation and how we grow as Christians through
stages, until we eventually come to full maturity.

I remember, many years ago, meeting a person who
had undergone gender reassignment and then had
come to know the Lord as Savior. This individual had
been born a male, but, after surgery, was now living
as a woman and was praying that God would do a
creative miracle and provide a uterus for childbear-
ing. Like myself, this new Christian had not yet
learned how to pray according to God's will and was
unaware that God would not answer certain prayers.

We are all ignorant in the early stages of our Christian walk, but as we grow in our knowledge of God's
Word, our prayers gradually became conformed to
His will. The Holy Spirit is our Teacher, and He will
lead us into all truth (see 1 John 2:27). If we "mess

up" and sin, God does not condemn us, but forgives and restores us to relationship, as we turn to Him (see 1 John 1:9). God is very quick to respond to new Christians, just as a mother quickly responds to the cry of her baby. She loves her child and wants the baby to feel safe and secure in the knowledge that she is near and can be relied upon. In like manner, our Father teaches us to trust Him until we become like a "*weaned child with its mother*" (Psalm 131:2), not fussing and fretting about having our needs met, but calm in the knowledge that every need is known and will be met at the appropriate time by Jehovah Jireh, the One who Provides. "*Be still, and know that I am God,*" He is saying to our hearts (Psalm 46:10).

Through these things, the Holy Spirit is drawing us to Himself, to reveal Jesus in an ever more intimate way:

> *My dove in the clefts of the rock, in the hiding places on the mountainside, show me your face, let me hear your voice; for your voice is sweet, and your face is lovely.* Songs of Songs 2:14

Intimacy with God cannot be developed quickly. It is a process, and it takes time. Those of us who want to get close to God might presume that everyone else does too, but this is not the case. Not everyone finds intimacy easy or enticing. Intimacy, for some people, is a frightening thing. To them, it smacks of being controlled and manipulated, transgressed or abused. Getting close is just too risky for some. They have been hurt and let down by loved ones far too often, and now they can only feel safe by keeping people at a distance. The sad thing about this is that those walls designed to keep people at bay also keep God from getting close to us. He wants to heal us of these fears.

As our intimacy with the Father grows, gradually He begins to teach us about authority. The more the self-life comes under the control of the Holy Spirit, the more the Spirit can exercise power through us. It is a gradual giving over, or death to self. When the Holy Spirit is in control of our lives, there will be a beautiful balance of power, of love and of self-discipline (see 2 Timothy 1:7).

The Lord does not overemphasize any one area, but rather the Spirit reveals the different aspects of God's character — love, power and order. The nine fruits of the Spirit balance the nine gifts of the Spirit; both are necessary. The bells and pomegranates which trimmed the hems of the priests' garments in the Tabernacle pointed to the time when the Holy Spirit would move in power in Christian believers, producing both spiritual fruit and spiritual gifts. The witness of the Holy Spirit always brings peace, as well as a coherent unity, and anything from God's Spirit will always agree with the Scriptures.

I vividly remember, early in my Christian walk, when I began to earnestly desire the spiritual gifts. I prayed and fasted, begged and pleaded. I wanted to function in the gifts just like I saw others doing in the Church. I kept up my pleading, until one day God gently told me that I should seek the Giver and not the gifts. He was concerned for relationship, and I was interested in other things.

Over a period of almost three years, I sought God diligently and sought to correct my wrong focus. Suddenly, one day, my prayers were answered, and the power of God came so mightily I was overwhelmed. I was not expecting the power of the Holy Spirit to be quite so powerful, and I didn't know what to do with it.

Nor was I expecting the persecution that followed. The closer we get to Jesus, the greater the persecution will become (see John 15:20). Religious spirits "come out of the woodwork" whenever the Holy Spirit comes in power.

I also learned, through all this, that it isn't necessary to beg and plead with God for the gifts He said He would give. I only needed to align my will with His.

In his book *Still Higher for the Highest*, Oswald Chambers beautifully describes how the baptism of the Holy Spirit changes us:

Not witnesses of what Jesus can do, that is an elementary witness, but "witness unto Me" — you will be instead of Me, you will take everything that happens, praise or blame, persecution or commendation, as happening to Me. No one can stand that unless he is constrained by the majesty of the personal power of Jesus. Paul says I am constrained by the love of Christ, held as in a fever, gripped as by a disease, that is why I act as I do; you may call me mad or sober, I do not care; I am after only one thing — to persuade men of the judgement seat of Christ and of the love of God. [11]

Can you just imagine the monumental threat to Satan of large numbers of Christian believers running around being "as Jesus" to the world? Satan will do anything to stop that kind of a witness. And yet, before Christ comes again, I believe we will see it.

Those of us who are passionate for Christ want the real thing. Going through the motions — praying, praising and trying to do what others do — is often just form without substance, and the time comes when we've had enough. We desperately want more; we want the real thing — the substance, not the form. But often, we do not know how to go about getting it.

Perhaps we tasted the presence of Jesus briefly and lost it and now want it back. Like the woman with the issue of blood (in Mark 5:25-29), we may be desperate. She had heard that Jesus was passing by, and she figured that if she could just get close enough to touch Him, she would be healed. She was desperate, so when Jesus passed by, she reached out and touched the hem of His garment and was instantly healed. Her faith drew from Jesus, and her need was met.

God has shown us the way to come into His presence. If we use the furniture in the Tabernacle of Moses as a guide, it will lead us directly into the manifest presence of God. We enter via the Brazen Altar, by having our sins washed away by the blood of Jesus. A clean heart gives access to God. We die daily (see Luke 9:23). Daily we come to the Laver to be washed and purified by God's Word. By the light of the Lampstand, the Holy Spirit gives us revelation, and the fire of God burns within us, as we fellowship with God and with each other, as we partake of the Bread of Life, on the Table of Shewbread.

A *Sweet Aroma* rises to God from the Altar of Incense, as we lift our hands in worship to pray, praise and intercede for the lost. We now stand at the Veil, beyond which is the Shekinah glory. In the Holy of Holies, Jesus takes us into that glory, as He receives our sacrifice of praise, for it is He who has removed the Veil, thus providing direct access to the Father. We now stand in the presence of God.

Just like the musicians in the orchestra, if we keep

our eyes on the Conductor, we will have unity of purpose, and, as members of the Body of Christ, we will synchronize beautifully as we follow Him. In this way, the Spirit of God will lead us to bring in the end-time harvest, to complete the Great Commission. We need to remember: there is an enemy of the harvest who will do anything he can to steal souls from Christ, by putting blockages in our pathway to limit our effectiveness. But we can combat such resistance and fulfill our calling by learning how to live the abundant life Jesus purchased for us. We can learn how to apply God's principles for successful living, breaking off every stronghold of the enemy and removing every mind-set that hinders our progress in God.

"The Spirit of the Lord is on me, because he has anointed me to preach good news to the poor. He has sent me to proclaim freedom for the prisoners and recovery of sight for the blind, to release the oppressed, to proclaim the year of the Lord's favor."

Luke 4:18

.

Five

&

Setting the Captives Free

*T*he purpose of Christ's ministry was to preach the Gospel to the poor, afflicted and brokenhearted, to heal those who were bruised and oppressed, to open the spiritual eyes of those blinded by the world and Satan and to proclaim freedom and salvation from Satan's domain, freedom from sin, fear and guilt (see Luke 4:18-19). Christ set us free that we might worship Him, serve Him and fulfill our destiny in God. If this is the case, why is it that, much of the time, we are not experiencing this wonderful freedom in our daily lives? How is it that our lives are often like a roller-coaster ride — up one minute and down the next, constantly subject to changing moods?

The truth is that Jesus has purchased freedom for us. It is already ours, but we need to learn how to walk in it. We need to know how to get it to work in our lives, just as when Joshua led the Israelites into the Promised Land. The land was theirs; God had given it to them; but in order to occupy all the land that was their God-given possession, they had to remove enemy tribes one at a time. In that way, with God leading them through each battle, they were successful and, eventually, had total peace.

Sometimes, when people are saved, they are set free immediately in some areas, but when problems persist, we wonder what we must do to be free. Unless we are released from bondage and oppression, we cannot fulfill our callings; we will not be able to walk as overcomers, living the victorious life Christ purchased for us. God has made it possible for us to live the abundant life Jesus promised, and there is no reason for us to be robbed. He has provided everything we need in order to lay hold of our covenant blessings.

The work of overcoming the things that impede our progress in Christ is an active work, not a passive one. Jesus said, *"From the days of John the Baptist until now, the kingdom of heaven has been forcefully advancing, and forceful men lay hold of it"* (Matthew 11:12). This is a fight of faith. The Kingdom of Heaven is taken hold of by those committed to breaking away from sinful practices and constantly exerting themselves to lay hold of the promises. The Kingdom of God, with all its blessings and power, is not for those who have little desire to seek God, who compromise with the world, seldom pray and neglect the Word. [1]

The Kingdom of God is about choices, about exercising our wills toward God. When we are experiencing the Kingdom of God, we will have *"righteousness, peace and joy in the Holy Spirit"* (Romans 14:17), but we must fight for it. We must also fight to maintain it. There is no such thing as cheap grace.

We are soldiers of Christ (see 2 Timothy 2:3), waging war (see 2 Corinthians 10:3), and we need to put on the full armor of God so that we can resist the devil's schemes (see Ephesians 6:11). We have no choice but to be constantly vigilant, or we will end up defeated and wonder why.

I am not suggesting that we must run around constantly screaming at the devil. Rather, we will live in victory and be protected if we make a choice to live in holiness, to be always rejoicing in Christ and to walk in unity with other believers. It is a matter of living offensively, not defensively.

Even though we are fighting a spiritual battle, not all the answers to our problems will necessarily be of a spiritual nature. We long for relief from emotional turmoil and long to find direction in our spiritual walk, but we often do not know where to look for the answers. Lack of understanding regarding the way God has made us is often behind such confusion.

Sometimes we lose sight of the different aspects

which come together to make us human. There are
five main areas of our lives that need to be considered when trying to get free from hindrances to our
progress: physical, emotional, intellectual, social and
spiritual. We might ask ourselves, "Is my problem
stemming from my physical health? Do I allow my
emotions to control me? Are my miseries due to the
way I think about the world, other people, myself or
God? Are my difficulties because of the way I com-
municate and relate to others? Or is my problem
arising from lack of or faulty understanding of God's
Word and God's ways?" These are all very good questions. Jesus tells us:

> " 'Love the Lord your God with all your heart
> and with all your soul and with all your strength
> and with all your mind'; and, 'Love your neigh-
> bor as yourself.' "   Luke 10:27

This verse of scripture mentions the five different
areas related to human functioning. In the Greek, the
word for "heart" is *kardia,* and it refers to the respon-
sive and emotional reactions we have as human
beings. [2] The Greek word for "soul" is *psyche,* which
refers to the vitality and consciousness of a person. [3]
Physical strength or might is *ischys* in the Greek, and
this refers to the powerful and instinctive drive we
have. [4] The Greek word for "mind" is *dianoia;* it refers

to our qualities of intelligence and planning — the capacity to think. [5]

Each part of our functioning influences the other parts, so that improvement in one area overflows to the others. It is not possible to separate the various elements of our humanness, because of the way they overlap, but it is helpful to look at the different areas in order to understand how to remove blockages.

I mentioned earlier that there are layers of woundedness which hinder our intimacy with God, and because His sole purpose is relationship, He desires to remove those barriers. If we are serious about our walk with the Lord, the Holy Spirit will begin to show us areas He wants to heal. He will bring them to the surface.

We can be comforted by the fact that God won't do it all at once; He will not overwhelm us. There is no need to run away and hide because a prophetic word has come that God wants to heal you and set you free. I have seen people terrified of what God might reveal to them or make them face. I have also seen others dump their problems in God's lap and walk away, expecting Him to fix everything, without their realizing that they had a part to play. We are to do our part, and God will do His. He won't do ours, and we can't do His.

There are no formulas to follow for divine governance; God's plan is given to us in principles, not specific details. The reason there are no precise rules to follow is that this is not an exact science. Rather, we are to be led by God's Spirit, step by step, in His unfolding plan for our individual lives. His ways are perfect, and His timing is perfect, so we can relax in His arms.

There are general principles for us to follow, some things we can do to help ourselves through.

Some problems are straightforward. For example, a married couple experiencing conflict may simply lack effective communication skills. If that is the case, their problem is located in the social area of functioning. An individual who has been experiencing headaches, mood swings and fatigue over a period of time may learn, upon medical examination, that the problem is not stress related, as first thought, but in fact, has an organic basis. Such a problem, obviously, has its origin in the area of physical functioning.

Some difficulties are much more complex. Consider individuals who strive for perfection in all they do and who judge themselves mercilessly for never attaining the desired standard. Depression usually follows such repeated failures. The problem is not depression, nor is it perfectionism. Way back in the dim past, some significant person has criticized or rejected these people, and the response has been for them to see themselves as unworthy, not good

enough, insignificant and lacking. Performance ori-
entation has become the focus for acceptance, as a
result.

In order to get free from the bondage of perfectionism, the real problem must be seen clearly and named
for what it is. Lasting release will not come just by
offering prayer for the symptoms of depression and
perfectionistic behavior. The spiritual bondage, with
its emotional fruit, will remain until those who have
hurt us are forgiven and released. The root cause must
come to light. The Holy Spirit will bring such revelation as we sincerely seek to please Him. The help of a
pastor or Christian counselor may be valuable at this
point, or God may reveal the true source as we personally read His Word and pray.

Once we understand the basis of our struggle, we
need to ask ourselves whether we genuinely want to
be set free. Sometimes, there is secondary gain from
having a problem. We might enjoy the attention we
receive from others and, therefore, be afraid we will
lose something important to us if we let go and receive healing. This may even be unconscious on our
part, yet it still hinders our surrender to God's plan
for us.

Can we trust Him? There can be many reasons why
it is difficult to let go of problematic behavior. Fear
of change, fear of responsibility and fear of consequences are just a few. Do we really want to be set
free, with all that entails?

Probably one of the most disappointing aspects of being involved in counseling work is that sometimes people do not make progress despite the insights gained and skills learned. Some individuals have not yet reached the point that they are willing to do what is needed to bring change, and no one else can do it for them. There seems to be a temporary relief experienced when they talk about their problems. For the time being, they have off-loaded their burdens ... or at least they think they have. In reality, nothing has changed; they have only rehearsed the tragedy one more time. The buildup of immediate tension was released, and this was mistaken for a solution. The source of the need is still there; it must be dug out and removed so that a permanent resolution can take place.

Once we are aware of the real problem causing our misery and hindering our progress in God, and have ascertained our readiness to remove it, we need to forgive all those who have contributed to the development of the problem in our lives and also to repent of wrong reactions we may have had. We may have been on the receiving end of some very cruel and unloving behavior by family members or significant people in our lives, and therefore forgiveness may not be easy — especially forgiveness from the heart (see Matthew 18:35). The steps of forgiveness should accompany an acknowledgment of the pain caused, and an opportunity should be taken to grieve the losses sustained and disappointments experienced. Otherwise, it is not real; it is just a ritual we go through — just empty words.

We then need to consider our responsibility to forgive. Jesus said:

> *For if you forgive men when they sin against you, your heavenly Father will also forgive you. But if you do not forgive men their sins, your Father will not forgive your sins.*
>
> Matthew 6:14-15

Many ask what it means to forgive. What is involved in the process? Some are of the opinion that in order to forgive someone they need to like that person and somehow excuse their behavior, while others think forgiveness means forgetting. Forgiveness begins with a choice, an act of the will to release another and not stand in judgment, nor seek revenge. Forgiveness begins with the humility to admit that we also commit sin and need forgiveness. It necessitates seeing ourselves as God sees us.

The dictionary describes three important elements in the act of forgiveness. These include canceling the obligation, pardoning the offender and ceasing from anger or resentment. [6] Whether we like the offender is not the issue, but rather that we recognize that God

alone has the wisdom to judge an individual's behavior, including his motives — the intent of the
heart.

Forgiveness is powerful. It is a gift God has given
to restore us, not only in relationships, but within
ourselves. When we choose to forgive others, our inner being returns to a state of rest, and the peace and
joy of the Lord can flow once again. Forgiveness starts
with an act of the will, and then God's grace will take
us the rest of the way.

God brought this lesson home to me one night several years ago, when I was extremely angry with one
of my teenage daughters. She had had a birthday
party, which did not go as planned. As I lay on my
bed, rigid with anger, trying to go to sleep, but still
wide awake, the Lord reminded me of the need to
forgive. I had done nothing wrong; she had. But I
was the one who had to let it go. I felt no warm, positive feelings about the situation, but I agreed with God
and made the choice to forgive. As soon as I said the
words, "I forgive," God's peace flooded my whole
being, and I fell asleep.

When we forgive, the devil cannot get a foothold
to destroy us in that particular area of our lives. We
are accountable for the choices we make, and when
we choose to agree with God and release someone
from judgment, Satan is defeated at that point, defeated by love in action. Forgiveness helps maintain
our mental balance.

I remember a young woman who came for counseling, desperately unhappy over problems within her marriage and employment and also within herself. As we talked, she admitted to being embittered against her mother, whom she saw as manipulative and controlling. This young woman, who professed to be a Christian, refused to forgive her mother, saying the pain was too great, and her mother did not deserve forgiveness. Needless to say, the anguish of this young lady continued; she got no relief from talking, nor from gaining insight. She was not ready to take the next step.

The Bible tells us that mercy triumphs over judgment (see James 2:13), but this young woman was still demanding justice, and was not ready to release mercy to her mother. God longed to flood the young woman with peace and heal her broken heart, but He was prevented from blessing her because she would not forgive. She kept her grudge, and she kept her pain. As a result, she continued being a victim.

Guilt separates, but forgiveness restores relationships. The story of Jacob and Esau is an example of this. Jacob usurped Esau's birthright and blessing and then fled to Haran, to his uncle Laban, afraid of what Esau might do to him (see Genesis 27:41-28:10). Many years later, Jacob returned to his homeland with his wives, children and possessions, as God had instructed him to do. However, he was still afraid of

Esau's anger, and so he sent a party ahead of the women and children with gifts to pacify Esau — in case he went on the attack (see Genesis 32:13-21). Then Jacob divided the people and animals into two groups, so that if Esau came and attacked one group, the other could escape. Jacob was filled with fear.

Jacob's fears were unfounded. Esau saw his brother coming and *"ran to meet Jacob and embraced him; he threw his arms around his neck and kissed him. And they wept"* (Genesis 33:4). Jacob had repented, and Esau had forgiven him. God had dealt with heart attitudes, and now reconciliation was possible.

Some Christians I've counseled over the years have admitted to me that they had never felt the need to forgive — even though they had experienced years of turmoil and pain as a result. These people had grown so accustomed to living in defeat and feeling miserable they had lost sight of God's way of restoration. God's way is so simple, yet if the devil can blind us to the way out of our dilemma, he will. He will target our vulnerabilities and apply constant pressure, to keep us defeated and ineffective — if we let him.

Sometimes, by not forgiving others, we bind people to certain behavioral patterns toward us. The moment we release them through the prayer of forgiveness, their behavior towards us is free to change. This has to do with ties in the spirit realm and is not simply an emotional or relational issue. We must not forget to forgive those who have abused us or let us down in a passive way, by neglecting us or by not preventing others from harming us. We may be just as angry with them as with the offender and yet be unaware of it. By holding such bitterness and angry judgments against them, we block both them and ourselves from the spiritual freedom that leads to emotional freedom. As we let go, we can begin to love with God's love, and such love always brings healing.

This is a process that may take time, but it begins with releasing others from judgment. That is forgiveness.

Just as I have seen people balk at the need to forgive those who have hurt them, so I have also seen countless others find release from emotional burdens, when they humbled themselves and forgave. Some also experience physical healings through the act of forgiveness.

Accompanying the need to forgive is the need to repent of wrong reactions to having been wounded. This includes ungodly attitudes or behavior we may have developed as a way of coping or of protecting ourselves in life. It seems to be the most natural thing in the world to put up walls to keep certain people out, when we've been let down by them. These walls of pride, which say, "I'm right," or of criticism, which say, "You're wrong," or perhaps of revenge, which say, "I'll make you suffer," will also keep God at a distance and rob us of peace. We may also have developed comfort behaviors which have led to addictions.

When he was inside the belly of the great fish, the prophet Jonah declared: *"Those who cling to worthless idols forfeit the grace that could be theirs"* (Jonah 2:8). Anything that comes before God, even our self-righteous attitudes, amounts to idolatry and steals God's grace from us. Not believing God's Word and what it says about us will rob us of the wholeness He wants to give us. We may need to repent and forgive ourselves also and cease playing the role of scapegoat and martyr. Then we can ask the Lord to set us free from all bondages and oppression through the power of the blood of Jesus.

As we take our spiritual authority and speak forth the word of faith, God will heal our wounded spirits and completely deliver us through the power of the Holy Spirit. It may be that the Spirit will reveal the need to pull down spiritual strongholds and cast out demons or perhaps to break vows that had been made many years earlier. Such vows act as curses, preventing freedom in the Spirit and contributing to ongoing emotional difficulties. It may also be necessary to renounce any involvement in witchcraft or occult practices before God can release us.

Getting set free is a work of the Holy Spirit, just as forgiveness and repentance are. The whole process is Spirit led, and all we need to do is cooperate. We exercise our divine authority, using the weapons of our warfare, remembering that our battle is not against people, but against the powers of darkness (see Ephesians 6:12). Of course, demonic spirits will use any available channel to discourage us, and sometimes the channel used may be a loved one or even people in the Church. As long as we keep turning to the Light, the works of darkness will be exposed.

As I stated in an earlier chapter, the conflicts we have with one another are mostly about getting our needs met, and many times we lack the grace to achieve that unselfishly. This can be a trap, for whenever there are old wounds, the enemy can defeat us. Satan will resist our getting healed, because he loses his influence to do damage at that point. It's a bit like termites eating away the internal structure of a building. When they are exposed to the light, they die. Exposing the works of darkness gives us the opportunity to stop the damage.

Once we have been released, we need to thank and praise God and pray that the Holy Spirit will fill all those empty places with Himself, with His peace and joy, and to guard the precious work that has been done.

> It is for freedom that Christ has set us free.
> Stand firm, then, and do not let yourselves be
> burdened again by a yoke of slavery.
>   Galatians 5:1

In order to stand firm and not be enslaved again, we need to heed Romans 12:2 and embark on renewing our minds, or aligning our thinking with God's Word. We need to be made new in the attitudes of our minds, to put off the old corrupted self and put on the new self, created to be like God in true righteousness and holiness (see Ephesians 4:23-24). Reading the Bible on a regular basis will help to conform us to God's ways, as the Holy Spirit speaks to us, and will alert us to the enemy's strategies. God will unfold to us His unconditional love and help us see our importance to Him and His plan.

As we continue to seek the Lord in prayer and walk obediently with Him, He may begin to show us new ways of doing things. He will show us how to exchange old defeating patterns for new ones.

The Holy Spirit may impress upon us the need to remove stress from our lives and live more simply. He may highlight the need to attend to nutrition or exercise or perhaps learn to set appropriate boundaries in relationships. We may be instructed by God to handle our finances differently. He might speak to us about the importance of tithing and show us that being obedient in this area opens the windows of Heaven over our lives for blessing (see Malachi 3:10).

I vividly remember a woman coming for financial assistance and emergency food relief to the inner-city mission where I was working as a volunteer a couple of years ago. She had a beautiful smile and openly talked about her faith in the Lord, even praising Him for the parking spot she'd managed to get in the busy street outside. At the end of the interview, the young woman inquired whether there was anything else she could do to improve her family's situation. I asked her if, as a Christian, she was tithing. She hung her head and confessed that all had been well up until three years earlier when her husband suggested she stop paying the tithe in order to save more money. It had been a downhill run ever since, with the family now dependent upon welfare handouts.

God is very practical, and He has created a material world. Not all solutions to emotional difficulties and unhappiness will be of a spiritual nature; some may be very practical. This is why we need the Holy Spirit's guidance. He knows how to strengthen us in the midst of trials and uncertainties.

While I have outlined some broad guidelines to emotional and spiritual freedom, it is important to point out that this is not a formula. The Christian life is lived by the power of the Son of God and is directed in all things by the Holy Spirit. The Scriptures tell us: *"Not by might nor by power, but by my Spirit," says the LORD Almighty* (Zechariah 4:6).

The power of the Spirit of God is able to break down any difficulty in our lives, no matter how great, and He will also supply the wisdom as to the best way to do it.

I was haunted by a fear of flying for many years. Although I traveled in airplanes, I was always extremely tense until we got back on the ground. I was anointed with oil by the elders of the church, I fasted, prayed, repented and claimed the promises of the Scriptures. I tried everything I knew to do, but to no avail. I continued to experience fear in this one, specific situation.

A few years ago, when I was planning to fly to the other side of the world to visit my daughter, the dreaded fear arose again. I was so "fed up" with feeling this way that I decided to search the Scriptures for a promise I could hold on to. I decided to use 1 Corinthians 10:13. If God has promised not to test us beyond what we are able to bear, I was ready to let go of the whole situation. At the moment I released faith in God's character, He completely removed my fear. I was totally delivered of all fear of flying, and that fear has not returned. Thus, I learned, through personal experience, that faith is needed to move the arm of God. Faith is not misplaced when it is faith in who His Word says He is, faith in His character.

I give this example to make the point that God alone knows the correct solution to every problem, and not all emotional pain is linked with unforgiveness. Sometimes, all we have to do to get free in a particular area is to simply obey something God is telling us to do. As long as we don't obey God's specific instructions to us, we remain bound. You may have forgiven and repented and still be troubled by problematic behaviors and emotions.

These things may be conditioned, that is, you have been trained to respond in certain ways to certain cues, just like puppies in dog-training school. What God may want to do is gradually "un-train" you, by exposing you to a whole new set of circumstances. He will then retrain you, to align your thinking with His Word, by gently loving you through the situations He personally orders for you.

Be patient and seek God for His strategy in each problem area. Remember Joshua.

A Summary of Key Principles

1. Recognize that there is a problem that God wants removed because it is a barrier to relationship with Him.
2. Define the true nature of the problem, not just the symptoms.
3. Ask yourself whether you are ready to accept the responsibility to do what is necessary to remove the problem and put structures in place to prevent it from returning.
4. Forgive all those who have contributed to the development of the problem in your life.
5. Repent of wrong attitudes and actions toward others, toward God and toward yourself. Anything

you have done independently of God in order to cope needs to be repented of and stopped.

6. Speak in faith, declaring all bondages and oppressions broken through the power of the blood of Jesus, cutting off all ongoing effects of past hurts and fears.

7. Give thanks and praise to God for all He has done, and ask Him to fill you afresh with the Holy Spirit. Ask also that His Spirit will heal the deep emotional wounds you have carried.

8. Take whatever steps are necessary to change negative thinking and behavior and put structures in place to support a positive lifestyle.

9. If you are still not free, after repentance and forgiveness, know that God may need to take you through a few things, until you are able to see what He is trying to show you. Trust His timing.

"I am the true vine, and my Father is the gardener. He cuts off every branch in me that bears no fruit, while every branch that does bear fruit he prunes so it will be even more fruitful. You are already clean because of the word I have spoken to you. Remain in me, and I will remain in you. No branch can bear fruit by itself; it must remain in the vine. Neither can you bear fruit unless you remain in me.

"I am the vine; you are the branches. If a man remains in me and I in him, he will bear much fruit; apart from me you can do nothing."

John 15:1-5

Six

❦

Fruitfulness

f you are a born-again believer in Jesus Christ, you have joined the army. Whether you are aware of it or not, you are a soldier of Christ, and as such, will be trained, disciplined and equipped to take up your post in God's Kingdom-building enterprise. Paul wrote to the Ephesians:

> *Your strength must come from the Lord's mighty power within you. Put on all of God's armor so that you will be able to stand safe against all strategies and tricks of Satan. For we are not fighting against people made of flesh and blood, but against persons without bodies — the evil rulers of the unseen world.*
> Ephesians 6:10-12, TLB

The armor of Christ (see Ephesians 6:10-18) is our

protection in battle, but we still need to be trained and disciplined to follow our Commander — the Lord Jesus Christ. It is through God's Spirit that we receive the Lord's instructions, and this is the reason it is important to know the sound of His voice. The Holy Spirit will lead us into a life of fruitfulness as we learn to understand God's ways and learn not to become disheartened in the difficult times.

The passage of scripture which introduces this chapter (John 15:1-5) makes it clear that we will bear fruit, then more fruit, then much fruit if we remain attached to the vine. This is the condition for fruitfulness in our lives — remaining attached to the vine, to Jesus.

Abundant fruit does not come straight away; it takes time and is a gradual process. Whatever fruit or effective ministry is produced in our lives, whether it is leading people to Christ or building up churches, the first fruit we will always see will be the fruit of the Spirit — love, joy, peace, patience, kindness, goodness, faithfulness, gentleness and self-control (see Galatians 5:22-23). Effective ministry flows from the Spirit.

The Lord is gentle and mindful of our weakness. When the Israelites crossed over the Jordan River into the Promised Land, God spoke to Joshua:

> *"See, I am sending an angel ahead of you to guard you along the way and to bring you to the place I have prepared.*

> *"My angel will go ahead of you and bring you*
> *into the land of the Amorites, Hittites, Perizzites,*
> *Canaanites, Hivites and Jebusites, and I will*
> *wipe them out.*
> *"But I will not drive them out in a single year,*
> *because the land would become desolate and the*
> *wild animals too numerous for you. Little by*
> *little I will drive them out before you, until you*
> *have increased enough to take possession of the*
> *land."*   Exodus 23:20, 23 and 29-30

As God did with Joshua, so will He do with us. Joshua and the fighting men won battle after battle, as they were led by God to gradually inhabit the Promised Land. As the tribes were defeated, the Israelites took their God-given inheritance. Eventually, they had total peace.

We, also, will come into our inheritance, as we systematically remove the things that are not of God from our lives — things like pride, independence, rebellion and anything we place before God. These are all idols.

> *"If you remain in me and my words remain in*
> *you, ask whatever you wish, and it will be given*
> *to you. This is to my Father's glory, that you*
> *bear much fruit, showing yourselves to be my*
> *disciples."*   John 15:7-8

The life and power of God will flow through us, as we clear the way. We are conduits for Jesus. We do nothing in our own strength; it is His life flowing through us. We are to reflect Him to the world. Just like the Israelites overcame their enemies, the Lord trains us also to overcome.

In order to overcome, we need faith and endurance. We can learn much about this from the great patriarchs of the Old Testament. When God called Abraham, He told him to leave his people and his country and go to an unknown destination, trusting God. God will often separate us from the comfort of familiar surroundings and supports for a time, in order to cause us to draw closer to Him and learn to depend upon Him more fully.

As Abraham obeyed, he received further revelation, and God continued to lead him. God told him that he would have many descendants and that his wife, Sarah, would be a *"mother of nations"* (Genesis 17:16). However, Sarah was barren and well advanced in age. It was twenty-five years before the birth of Isaac and the fulfillment of the promise.

Twenty-five years is a long time. Abraham believed God, but after about ten years of waiting, he and Sarah began to wonder if they were supposed to help God out in bringing this promise to pass. According to the custom in Mesopotamia, a barren wife would have her handmaid bear children for her. So Hagar,

Sarah's maid, gave birth to Ishmael. In the New Testament, Hagar's son is likened to human effort, because he was born in the ordinary way, while Isaac was born in God's way and came in God's timing through the power of the Holy Spirit.

Waiting for God's timing can be confusing, and like Abraham and Sarah, we can be mistaken also and attempt to provide a way for God to fulfill His promises to us. Human effort, however, always complicates circumstances, and we end up paying a price. In Abraham's case, the price he paid for his mistake was that Ishmael persecuted Isaac, just as the sons of the flesh today continue to persecute the sons of the Spirit (see Galatians 4:29). Abraham was human, and he made mistakes, but he was a man of great faith. We see that in the way he obeyed God and offered up Isaac as a sacrifice, when God was testing his faith.

God's covenant with Abraham extended to his son of promise, Isaac, but Isaac's wife, Rebekah, was also barren. So Isaac prayed and asked the Lord for children. It took twenty years of prayer and endurance of faith before the twins, Jacob and Esau, were born.

God's covenant extended to Jacob, but his wife, Rachel, was barren, like Rebekah and Sarah before her. In her desperation, Rachel cried out, *"Give me children or I'll die"* (Genesis 30:1, TLB). Many years would pass, however, before she gave birth to Joseph.

Even though the promise of many descendants was

given to Abraham as part of his covenant relationship with God, there were still many barriers that had
to be removed in his and succeeding generations. Attaining the promise required continued prayer, faith,
obedience and perseverance. God's grace and God's
timing were also essential in bringing about His plan.

Another of the great men of faith was Moses. God
took eighty years to prepare this leader before he had
the character qualities necessary to accomplish the
task to which God was calling him. We often sense
God's calling and step out too soon, just as Moses
did. Somehow, Moses knew he was called to be the
deliverer of his people, and so, at the age of forty, he
reached out to help one of his countrymen being attacked by an Egyptian. Things went horribly wrong,
as they do for us when we are out of God's timing. As
a result, God sent Moses out into the desert for another forty years, in order to teach him humility and
dependence.

In God's perfect timing, He called Moses supernaturally from a burning bush, to lead the Israelites out
of captivity in Egypt (see Exodus 3:2). God had prepared Moses, called him unmistakably and placed
power and authority upon him in a most remarkable
way to accomplish the task. It is important for us to
be aware that authority from God is released only to
those whose activity originates from God and who
are energized by God. Only what is spoken with God's

authority will touch our spirits and motivate us to take the necessary steps of obedience that will change lives. All else touches the intellect and emotions and amounts to dead works. Only the Spirit gives life.

Another of the great heroes of faith was Joseph, whose life was one of endurance and faithfulness in the midst of injustice (see Genesis 37-50). He learned dependence on God in the face of futility. But Joseph was able to hang on when the going was rough, because God had prepared him, just as He will prepare you and me for the trials ahead.

God had given Joseph two dreams to provide revelation and faith for his difficult future. He dreamed that his brothers' sheaves of wheat bowed down to his sheaf of wheat and also that the sun, moon and eleven stars bowed down to him (see Genesis 37:7-9). He knew God was taking him somewhere.

Joseph was a key part of God's plan that was far broader in scope than one man's life, and yet the details of his life were very important to the success of the plan. Joseph is seen as having a special vocation as preserver of the covenant family, until the time of deliverance under Moses. Although Joseph was innocent, he was treated cruelly and rejected, receiving undeserved blame and punishment.

Sold to passing Ishmaelite traders by his brothers, who were jealous of him, Joseph was taken to Egypt. There, he was sold as a slave to Potiphar, an officer

of Pharaoh and captain of the guard. Joseph pros-
pered in Potiphar's house, because the Lord was with
him, and he was entrusted with great responsibility.
Joseph earned trust and respect over a period of time,
by living in a godly way.

The time came, however, when Joseph was greatly
tested in another way. Potiphar's wife showed interest in the lad and tempted him to have a sexual
relationship. It is important to realize that Joseph was
alone in a foreign country and separated from loved
ones and people who cared. He had no emotional
support whatsoever. Still, Joseph resisted.

We cannot say that we have been tempted until
there is an unmet need in our lives and the possibility of meeting that need, independent of God, comes
along. A person's life may appear to be above re-
proach, but this may only be because he or she has
not yet been tempted in certain areas. God will allow
particular trials to come our way, specifically to bring
to the surface wrong attitudes we did not know were
there. For this reason, we need to have humility regarding the sins and failures of others.

Even though Potiphar's wife harassed Joseph, he
continued to resist temptation. Satan will harass us
also where we are most vulnerable. Joseph was wrong-
fully accused of approaching Potiphar's wife sexually
and was subsequently imprisoned. Death would normally have been the penalty for such an offense by a

foreigner, but we see God's providence in the lesser penalty.

While Joseph seemed to be going from one disaster to another, he was actually safe in the hands of Almighty God, for he had been chosen by God and was being prepared to play a part in history. We also have been chosen to accomplish God's purposes, and when that reality grips us, we can take pressure, delay, opposition or hindrance.

Joseph's integrity cost him everything. While salvation is free, preparation for spiritual authority is very costly and difficult. God tests us with fire: *"The crucible for silver and the furnace for gold"* (Proverbs 17:3). Our lives will be refined like precious metal. When the heat is applied, the impurities come to the surface; they are exposed so they can be removed, and what is left is usable.

While Joseph was in prison, the Lord was with him and granted him favor in the eyes of the prison warden, who put him in charge of prison affairs. Pharaoh's chief cupbearer and baker were imprisoned along with Joseph. When they had dreams they could not understand, Joseph explained their meanings. The Lord gave him success in all he did.

It is not difficult to see the ministry of Joseph operating already, in its early stages, behind prison bars. He had administrative ability, could manage people and was trusted with responsibility. Among his God-given talents, Joseph must have had good communication skills, as well as a certain amount of wisdom and humility. But Joseph wasn't perfect; he still needed training.

The baker was beheaded, but the cupbearer was released from prison back into his position in Pharaoh's household. Before he left, Joseph asked him:

> *"When all goes well with you, remember me and show me kindness; mention me to Pharaoh and get me out of this prison. For I was forcibly carried off from the land of the Hebrews, and even here I have done nothing to deserve being put in a dungeon."*   Genesis 40:14-15

Joseph was human, like the rest of us, and was still learning his lessons of dependence upon God. He momentarily forgot that God is sovereign and in control of what comes our way, and He does not need our flesh to help Him bring His purposes to pass. That little mistake cost Joseph another two years in prison, as he learned to trust that release comes in God's perfect timing. [1]

When Pharaoh had a dream that troubled him, the cupbearer remembered Joseph, who, by now, was prepared by God to come from obscurity into the fulfillment of His promises. Joseph had been through the fire and was now a vessel fit for God's use. He had been tested and tried and found faithful. When Pharaoh asked Joseph to interpret his dream, Joseph replied, *"I cannot do it, but God will give Pharaoh the answer he desires"* (Genesis 41:16).

Joseph did not touch God's glory, and he refused to glory in the flesh. He had reached the end of himself, and he knew that, within himself, there was no good thing, no righteousness of his own. At this point of spiritual maturity, God released Joseph into great authority and great honor, by placing him as governor over the whole land of Egypt, second only to Pharaoh, in order to store food for the coming famine. Only humility could handle such exaltation. Joseph had been seventeen years old when he was sold into slavery in Egypt, and he was now thirty. He had been in training for thirteen years. *yes. Soul*

When God has finished fashioning the vessels He intends us to be, He brings us out of the furnace. We've been fired and are now ready for use. The time of testing our faith has come to an end. God has established our faith; it has become firm, and He can see that throughout our trials we were *"not moved from the hope held out in the gospel"* (Colossians 1:23). When we come to the end of the trial of our faith, we know it; we are not left wondering. Graduating from the fiery furnace is accompanied by abundant blessings, rest and promotion.

Joseph's preparation had begun with two dreams, or visions, which, in due time, were literally fulfilled. What looked like a promising future from the dreams appeared to die a natural death, when he was taken away to Egypt to a life of slavery. Joseph endured the trials he passed through by maintaining faith and integrity. He could have disqualified himself again and again, but he lived in his spiritual anointing, using his spiritual gifts, and came out of the furnace in intimate communion with God. At the point of his release, Joseph began to serve his God by serving his king and his nation.

Joseph had gained wisdom throughout his trials. There will be an increase in wisdom, as there is an increase in holiness, and Joseph had borne fruit unto holiness, which was to last throughout eternity (see Romans 6:22).

Joseph held no resentment towards those who had meant him harm; he was forgiving. He did not wallow in self-pity while he was in difficult circumstances. Rather, he bore fruit by steadfastly maintaining a strong stance of faith, even while in Potiphar's house and in prison, and despite all the restriction he had suffered.

There are three layers to Joseph's story, that is, several purposes. God had an overall plan for Israel that through the Davidic line would come the Messiah, the Savior of the world. It was through the tribe of

Judah (one of Joseph's older brothers) that Jesus came. At the local level, it was Joseph whom God used to keep the small remnant nation alive in time of famine and to bring them down to Egypt in fulfillment of God's promise to Abraham. God was revealed as Almighty Sovereign and Provider in meeting the needs of the people for food. These were evangelistic purposes for Egypt and the surrounding nations. The details of Joseph's life were extremely important to the fulfillment of God's plans, and we can see God's ways in preparing and orchestrating circumstances all along the way to achieve His purposes through Joseph at the critical time.

In Joseph's life, we see suffering that had redemptive purposes. This kind of suffering, which brings undeserved blame and accusation, is what God uses to mold us. He allows us to experience the same kind of humiliation that Jesus suffered. And God desires that we learn to develop the same response that Jesus did, to love unconditionally and to live in continual forgiveness, despite opposition.

Jesus *"learned obedience from what he suffered"* (Hebrews 5:8). He learned dependence upon His Father. He said, *"By myself I can do nothing"* (John 5:30). Jesus is our model for humility and dependence upon God, and we can see how God trained Joseph in this, as we trace his life story.

God will not release a believer for a ministry of

power and authority because he or she has a great personality, is well-educated, is well-connected or fasts and prays a lot. There is only one way for us to be anointed with power and learn to exercise the authority Christ purchased for us, and that is by passing through the "fire of affliction."

This process is painful, exquisitely painful, and it will test us to the breaking point. Just as God tested Abraham, to see if he was a covenant-keeping man, by asking him to kill his own son (the most precious thing to his heart), so likewise God will require us to let Him put His hand upon what is most precious to us. It would not be a painful affliction if it was not the closest thing to our hearts. There is no need to be afraid of what God will do; He is perfect in all His ways; He loves us perfectly, and *"perfect love casts out fear"* (1 John 4:18, NKJ). God is not capricious and will not play havoc with our lives. We don't know where the area of need is in our lives, until God turns the heat on us and reveals it to us through circumstances.

Within any local Christian congregation, there are people at different stages of their walks with the Lord. Some will be new believers, without much understanding yet, of God's ways. Others will be well and truly immersed in the "fire of affliction," while others are ready to be released by God in power and authority, to serve in their God-given callings. All are producing fruit at their different stages of development.

At some stage, we all ask the question, "What am I, God?" "What have You made me to be?" "What is my gift?" There are a few things we can do to help gain understanding of where we fit into the Body of Christ, but God tends to shield us from seeing too much, probably because if we knew what He was planning, we would try to help Him achieve it. We are notorious for that. Aside from that, we live by faith, and our whole task as Christians consists in hearing the voice of God's Spirit and doing what He says — no more and no less.

We can, however, get an idea of where we fit in, by looking at the gifts God has given us (see Ephesians 4:11, Romans 12:3-8 and 1 Corinthians 12). Our motivational gifts are always operating, whether we realize it or not, and we can further explore this area by reading some of the helpful books available.

It also helps to know there are stages of growth we pass through in our Christian walk, so we can gauge where we are on our journey. These stages parallel the stages of human growth and development toward maturity in a large way. From the time of birth to the age of six years is a foundational stage in our lives, in which we receive love and discipline. From six to twelve is a training stage, in which we focus on gathering information and learning to create. From twelve to twenty, we learn self-control and develop skills. From twenty to thirty, we begin to become productive and serve an apprenticeship, where we help others to be a success. From thirty to fifty, we are productive in our field of work and exert some influence. From fifty onwards, we are able to give counsel and guidance to others. Finally, the heritage stage is the latter part of our lives, when we focus on what we will leave behind after death.

The time God takes to bring us from the early stages of being babies in Christ to the moment in which He anoints us with power for fruitful service will depend on how quickly we surrender our wills to Him and die to self-ambition. For the seed must first fall into the ground and die before it can bring forth the grain, *"first the stalk, then the head, then the full kernel in the head"* (Mark 4:28). There are three successive stages of growth, or change, described here, and we see this pattern again and again throughout the Scriptures.

Jesus went through three stages, receiving three different baptisms, before He eventually ministered in power. First, He was baptized by John in the Jordan (see Matthew 3:13-15), signifying death to self and commitment to God's will. Then He was baptized by the Holy Spirit (see Matthew 3:16). He was then led into the wilderness for forty days of testing. This was His fire of affliction before His anointing of power.

King David also received three anointings. The first anointing came when he was young and still in training (see 1 Samuel 16:13). He then struggled with King

Saul hunting him down and hounding him with false accusations, before his second anointing as king over Judah (see 2 Samuel 2:4). David's third anointing was as king over all of Israel (see 2 Samuel 5:3).

Spiritual maturity is often symbolized by three levels of progression. The number three is important in scripture as it signifies "divine completeness," and we see that God tends to emphasize spiritual truths three times. For example, the Outer Court, Inner Court and Most Holy Place of the Tabernacle led from initial salvation through to the very presence, or glory, of God. The existence of the milk of the Word, the bread of the Word and the meat of the Word also teaches us that we move through stages in our spiritual understanding, from babies, to adolescents, to mature adults.

> *"But the one who received the seed that fell on good soil is the man who hears the word and understands it. He produces a crop, yielding a hundred, sixty or thirty times what was sown."*
> Matthew 13:23

Here we see three levels of output that are possible. We see fruit, more fruit and much fruit. We have a choice as to whether we yield thirty-, sixty- or a hundredfold with what God gives us. We can stop at thirty and settle down, or we can move on through the testings to produce sixtyfold. If we choose to go all the way with God, then we will pass through the fire, which will bring us to the hundredfold anointing, where we become mature.

Just as Jesus was humiliated and went to the cross, to die, and then was raised in resurrection power, so also, we are required to identify with Christ, be humiliated and experientially (in the circumstances of our lives) go to the cross and die to our own desires regarding those circumstances.

While Jesus has legally taken away Satan's power, we have to walk it out in our lives. It doesn't happen automatically. This is the point of power for us; this is where we gain the authority over the devil in our lives. If we can die to self at the most painful place in our lives, then Satan can no longer influence us, to hold us captive; he is defeated at that point. *"They overcame him by the blood of the Lamb, and the word of their testimony"* (Revelation 12:11). This will be our testimony of overcoming, where it has cost us the most. When God sees that we choose to keep the covenant and give Him our best gift, in exchange for all He is and has, then He raises us in resurrection power.

The reason this is so important is that here, at this point, we triumphantly overcome. Our victory stems from conquering this area of weakness that could arise to be a snare of the enemy. God cannot trust us with spiritual power if we are open to spiritual attack at our most vulnerable point. With God, the means is the end, to a large extent. God does intend to promote us from one assignment to the next, as He did with Joseph. However, since His primary goal for us is relationship, the end, as far as God is concerned, is dependence upon Him. This dependence gives us great security, and we find we are at rest in God, just like Jesus was when He slept through the storm. If we humble ourselves under God's mighty hand, He will lift us up in due time (see 1 Peter 5:6).

This important lesson is powerfully demonstrated to us in the story of Joshua and the Israelites crossing the Jordan River into the Promised Land to receive their inheritance. *"The men of Reuben, Gad and the half-tribe of Manasseh crossed over, armed, in front of the Israelites, as Moses had directed them"* (Joshua 4:12). It is very significant that God said these three tribes should lead the nation into their inheritance, for the names Reuben, Gad and Manasseh have significant meanings. Jedediah Tham has an insightful approach to this teaching. He suggests that these three names reveal to us the three conditions which are necessary in our lives before we can come into our inheritance.

Reuben was the firstborn son of Jacob and, as such, should have received a double portion of blessings, which was the Hebrew tradition. However, Reuben had lost his inheritance because of sin. The name *Reuben*, in Hebrew, indicates "disqualification as a son," so Reuben had to prove he was a son. [2] God demands that we prove our sonship in order to qualify for our spiritual inheritance (covenant blessings). In the Greek, there are two kinds of sons: *teknon*, meaning an immature child of God, who enjoys God's blessings by grace (see Galatians 4:1-3), and *huios*, a mature child of God who has received his inheritance by approval (see Galatians 4:5). [3] The mature child of God has reached adulthood in spiritual stature and has proven character. The *teknon*, or immature child, must remain under tutors and governors until he or she has grown up.

The kind of persecution Joseph suffered, as he was being brought to maturity by God, is the same kind we will suffer. For as coheirs with Christ, we must suffer with Him in order to reign with Him (see Romans 8:17). It may be a boss at work, a relative or a neighbor who will falsely accuse and blame us, but behind these tutors, God is working out His plan in our lives. If we squirm out of the situations God orders for us and resist the changes He is trying to make, then we remain childish, just like a servant who lives in the same house, but is not an heir to the father's property.

The prodigal son is a classic example of a childish Christian trying to lustfully claim his father's inheritance. [4] We can be disqualified from our covenant blessings because we refuse to grow up. God requires that we grow from *teknon* to *huios* before we can be trusted with all things in Christ. It is the Holy Spirit who places children of God, *teknon*, born ones, as adult sons in a legal standing before God and in relationship to Him. [5] In other words, when the time comes for us to be released in power and authority, like Joseph was, this will be God's doing. It is the way we live that demonstrates to God our mature sonship.

The name *Gad*, in the Hebrew, means "to overcome, to be an invader." It is forceful people who lay hold of the Kingdom of God with all its blessings (see Matthew 11:12). Spiritual violence, or militancy, is needed in order to obtain our inheritance in Christ, because it is very costly. When we walk the Calvary road, we walk it alone, and no one else can overcome for us. We must learn to stand on our own two feet — spiritually speaking. [6]

The name *Manasseh*, in the Hebrew, means "you must forget." We must learn to forgive and make a choice not to live as victims in life. We must learn to not allow our past to disqualify us from our inheritance in God. [7]

So, as we look at the three tribes that God chose to lead the Israelites into Canaan, we can see the conditions that God says are necessary before He will allow us to reach our spiritual potential. Reuben had to prove that he had character. Gad had to show he could stand on his own two feet and go through difficulties in life. And Manasseh had to learn to forgive, to let go of his hurts and get on with life. When these three conditions are present, everything else will follow.

W. Phillip Keller puts it very well, when he says:

> *We are given the free-will choice to decide for ourselves at which level of spiritual attainment we shall live in our walk with God. We can walk in the wilderness of divided loyalties and divided affections until the day we die. We can settle down easily just a short way from the life of conquest and victory to be content with only a distant view of our inheritance in Christ. Or, with courage, faith and joy in the Lord, we can enter fully into the victory and rest intended for us by our Father.* [8]

For Christ, the most exquisitely painful thing He could conceptualize was to be rejected by His Father, and yet if He was to become sin for us, then momentarily, that had to happen. He sweated blood in the Garden of Gethsemane, as He was tortured with His Father's request to surrender to His will and relinquish self-ambition at this point. He overcame, died to self and went to the cross. Consequently, God raised Him in resurrection power.

The Lord does not ask anything of us that He Himself has not suffered and overcome. He went before us and made the way.

Joseph exercised the spiritual gift of interpreting dreams throughout his time of preparation, as well as administrative gifts, but God was not finished with him yet. He was already bearing fruit, but God intended that Joseph would bear much fruit and come into a time of great expansion and influence in his calling. So God kept the pressure on Joseph until He could see the lad's heart was where it needed to be, until He could trust Joseph with his new assignment.

While God is dealing with us, doors will shut, and there will be delays and obstacles, as well as times when God withdraws. This withdrawal of God's voice is often referred to as "the dark night of the soul," and is a painful time of testing. Sometimes, the anointing for the spiritual gifts may be withdrawn for a time, so God can see how we react. Will we throw a tantrum and sulk when we see Christians who are less mature than us flowing in the anointing, while we are on the back burner, seemingly marking time? In all this, the Lord desires to bring us to the place Job reached when he said, *"Though he slay me, yet will I trust in him"* (Job 13:15, KJV). As Habakkuk said:

> *Though the fig tree does not bud and there are no grapes on the vines, though the olive crop fails and the fields produce no food, though there*

*are no sheep in the pen and no cattle in the
stalls, yet I will rejoice in the* LORD, *I will be
joyful in God my Savior.*

Habakkuk 3:17-18

Continual praise and thanksgiving for who God is
will bring us through our darkest hours. As we minister to the Lord in praise, the Holy Spirit will minister
joy and peace to us, and the joy of the Lord will be
our strength.

Then he brought me back to the door of the Temple. I saw a stream flowing eastward from beneath the Temple and passing to the right of the altar, that is, on its south side. Then he brought me outside the wall through the north passageway and around to the eastern entrance, where I saw the stream flowing along on the south side [of the eastern passageway].

Measuring as he went, he took me 1,500 feet east along the stream and told me to go across. At that point the water was up to my ankles. He measured off another 1,500 feet and told me to cross again. This time the water was up to my knees. Fifteen hundred feet after that it was up to my waist. Another 1,500 feet and it had become a river so deep I wouldn't be able to get across unless I were to swim. It was too deep to cross on foot.

He told me to keep in mind what I had seen, then led me back along the bank. And now, to my surprise, many trees were growing on both sides of the river!

He told me: "This river flows east through the desert and the Jordan Valley to the Dead Sea, where it will heal the salty waters and make them fresh and pure. Everything touching the water of this river shall live. Fish will abound in the Dead Sea, for its waters will be healed. Wherever this water flows, everything will live."

Ezekiel 47:1-9, TLB

Seven

❧

Life in the River

*I*n Ezekiel's vision, he describes seeing a stream of water flowing from the Temple. First, it is ankle-deep, then knee-deep, then waist-deep, then it becomes a river no one can cross, a river deep enough to swim in. This river brings life wherever it flows, and along its banks are trees with healing properties, and large numbers of fish live in the river, because it makes salt water fresh. This river speaks of abundant life, healing, peace and prosperity flowing from God to the land and the people. All this is made available through the power of the Holy Spirit. [1] Jesus said:

> *"Whoever believes in me, as the Scripture has said, streams of living water will flow from within him."*   John 7:38

These rivers described by Jesus refer to the Holy

Spirit and the blessing of abundant life He brings. All over the world, we are hearing about the movement of the Holy Spirit, with pockets of revival breaking out here and there. Books are being written describing the outpouring of God's Spirit, bringing salvation, healing and deliverance, accompanied by such manifestations as laughter, visions, shaking, groaning and much more. [2] Recently, we are hearing reports of gold dust falling in meetings, gold or silver fillings appearing in people's teeth and oil appearing on people's hands, faces and heads. [3] Some of these manifestations have accompanied revivals in previous centuries, so we should not be too surprised when they come upon us. We need to be aware of what God is doing and ready to receive all He wants to give us, for He is pouring out His Holy Spirit in the most amazing ways.

God has a way of coming unexpectedly and doing things that surprise us, in answer to prayer. On the Day of Pentecost, the Scriptures record, as the people were gathered together praying and seeking God, suddenly there was a sound like the blowing of a violent wind, and the people saw what seemed to be tongues of fire come to rest on each of those present (see Acts 2:2-3). God gave no warning of His intention, but sent His Holy Spirit in a most unusual way, a way the people had not experienced before.

So it was, for me, in mid-1998. On Mother's Day,

in May 1998, I went forward at church to bring a prophetic word. As I began to speak, the presence of God came upon me as a heavy weight and pushed me to the floor. The pastor followed me to the floor with the microphone, until I had finished speaking.

God's presence did not lift, however, and I found myself completely unable to move. I was sprawled in front of the pulpit and remained there for another hour or so, while the congregation continued worshiping. I remember being vaguely aware of many people stepping over me when they came forward to bring their tithes.

People often have visions when in this kind of state. I was aware of seeing a huge waterfall, something like Victoria Falls in Zimbabwe, and it formed a huge, forceful river. I was aware that this represented God's love being poured out to us in full force and coming in power to save, heal and set free. It was God's abundant blessings being showered on the nations.

Eventually, I was moved and carried to the back of the church by a couple of strong young men, because we had a visiting speaker that day, and I guess it seemed good manners to remove me from in front of his feet. I believe it was the Lord's wisdom, for no sooner had I been laid on the floor between the seats than the power of God increased, and I found my legs suddenly being jerked up and down, as I writhed, panted and groaned. My body appeared to be symbolically giving birth. I was shocked by all of this! I had never heard of such a thing and was completely unaware that intercessors before me had experienced this phenomenon. Not long after this, I was encouraged when I heard a pastor share his testimony and tell that he had also experienced a symbolic birthing process, and was shocked and unprepared for the way in which the Holy Spirit had overpowered him.

I was carried to my car three hours after this event, driven home and helped inside, so heavy was God's presence. Four days later, at about 11 AM, I was in my office at work, counseling, when suddenly, the same heavy weight of God's presence descended upon me, so that I could not sit upright. I began to slide sideways and laugh as I went. The woman I was counseling at the time wanted to know why I was laughing, but I found I could not speak properly. I managed to explain that I could not function, as God's presence had come upon me.

I was becoming more drunk in the Holy Spirit by the minute. I remember crawling across the floor to lay hands on her so that she might receive some of what I was getting. Eventually, she went out and told the secretary that I needed help. I could not stand, I could not sit and I could not talk.

The next client I was to see was a new one, a gentleman I had never met before. He arrived and sat in the waiting room, while I rolled around laughing on my office floor, pleading with God to allow me to function. Eventually, I pulled myself upright and walked out to the waiting room. Although I burst out in muffled laughter a couple of times, I managed to get him seated in my office. I had no idea what to do next, as I clung to the sides of my chair. I must have looked like a drunken person trying to stand up. The presence of God was so strong in the room that the gentleman got saved in the first twenty minutes, and his addiction to gambling was broken. He returned for two more visits, having found peace for the first time in his life, and God sovereignly reunited his family.

The presence of the Holy Spirit remained with me until about 8:30 that night. I was puzzled as to what I had given birth to, and when I asked God, He simply said, "The thing you have been praying for over the last twenty years." I had been asking God to come and supernaturally heal people's emotional wounds, to set them free and reclaim the ground stolen by the enemy, to make them whole by the power of His Spirit. I had been baptized in the Holy Spirit now for more than twenty years and was familiar with the anointing that came with the prophetic gifts. But this was different. This was new. God had taken twenty years to answer my prayers, but suddenly, He had come in a most unexpected way and begun to do as I had asked.

Sometimes the Holy Spirit comes to bring clarification through a prophetic word. Other times, He brings revelation by retrieving long forgotten information vital to a person's healing. There are times when God's presence fills my office, and the Holy Spirit moves powerfully to dislodge demonic spirits behind certain emotional and behavioral patterns, to break bondages. Still other times, the Lord comes with tears of compassion over the pain of His people.

Jesus knows just the right key to use to unlock a person's heart. Then, after He has set them free, He fills them with His Spirit. Some go out laughing uncontrollably, while others become so relaxed they want to fall asleep. God is bringing His people out of prison, and He is doing it in His own way.

I was not aware that God had not finished with me yet and that these strange manifestations were about to get stranger. I found myself giving birth on the floor of the church two more times over the next few months, and each time God added a new dimension to this new anointing. What felt like an electric current began to rush into my hands or arms, and I would begin to shake violently. At other times, my whole body would jerk and shake, accompanied by loud groaning. About a year later, oil began to ooze from my hands.

I have spent much time wondering what this was all about, knowing that, in scripture, there are many stories which demonstrate God's ingenuity in grab-bing the attention of His appointed audience. For example, He told Ezekiel He would make his tongue stick to the roof of his mouth and that he was to lie on his side and shave his head (see Ezekiel 3-5). All of this was to get the attention of sinful Israel.

Hosea was told to marry a prostitute as a message to the nation of Israel regarding her own spiritual prostitution from God. In the New Testament, the deaths of Ananias and Sapphira were very clear mes-sages about the seriousness of lying to the Holy Spirit (see Acts 5:3-10). Sometimes, actions speak louder than words, and many times, God's actions are symbolic.

It is important to understand what the Scriptures say about the things God does:

> *"For my thoughts are not your thoughts, nei-ther are your ways my ways," declares the* LORD. *"As the heavens are higher than the earth, so are my ways higher than your ways and my thoughts than your thoughts."*   Isaiah 55:8-9

In the book of Acts, we read of people who were amazed and perplexed with what they saw happen-ing on the Day of Pentecost. Some made fun of the disciples, as they saw them speaking in other tongues, presuming them to be drunk (see Acts 2:12-13). God does things we don't understand, and it may ruffle our feathers and cause us to think.

More than anything, we need discernment. We don't want to presume certain things are not of God and, as a result, forfeit the blessings that could have been ours. On the other hand, we need the ability to discern the difference between the flesh, the devil and the Holy Spirit. This is not always easy, especially when there is a mixture. I sometimes think God keeps us wondering in order to keep us humble. Who would have thought that the Creator of the universe would come to us in the form of a baby? Many very intelligent people missed that one!

As a result of these happenings over the past two years, I have come to see more clearly and experience more powerfully the amazing love that God has for us — believers and nonbelievers alike. I have come to see that Jesus really does want to come and sup with us (see Revelation 3:20). The Holy Spirit wants to take center stage and enter into every sphere of our lives. God wants to take over. Not only does He want to turn the Church upside down and change our values, but He wants to enter our places of work, and He wants to visit our homes and meet the needs of our families. He wants to make us happy. He really does!

A few weeks after the visitation from God in church and then in my office, similar things began to happen at home. To my surprise, the presence of the Holy Spirit began to come at the most unexpected times, to meet the needs of family members, in ways I never knew were possible.

One day, I went upstairs into my daughter Sarah's room to ask if she was planning to be home for dinner. As I entered her bedroom, the presence of God suddenly filled her room, and we were both overwhelmed as the Holy Spirit began to speak to her through a prophetic word. The Lord spoke so gently and personally to her that she recommitted her life to Him that day and has been walking with Him since. I left her room about an hour after I had entered, and I had gone in simply to see how many potatoes I should bake.

A few weeks later, I was getting ready for work one morning when the phone rang. I picked it up to hear our youngest daughter, Laura, screaming on the other end of the line. She was in Sydney, and had just had an accident and broken the bones in her foot. I could hear her saying her little toe was hanging at right angles to her foot. Suddenly, God's presence came in power and filled the kitchen where I was standing. I cried out to the Lord for healing, and after a few seconds, the screaming stopped. I heard Laura say, "The pain's gone."

Laura was in a difficult situation. She was staying on the eleventh floor of an apartment block, was new in the city, was all alone, could not walk and had to wait until her fiancé, Johann, could come and take her to a doctor. She was not able to phone him because he was shopping and knew nothing of her plight. She just had to wait. God graciously removed all pain, while she waited patiently to be rescued. It was discovered later that the bone was broken in three places. The pain never returned, and the foot healed perfectly.

Sometime later, I was talking on the phone to a friend in Sydney. We had chatted for about thirty minutes, and she was sharing how God had revealed an area in her life where she needed to be set free in order to progress in her ministry. As she was speaking, the same anointing of the Holy Spirit came as previously, and my friend became quiet as she heard me groaning. The Lord began to show me how to pray, and as I followed the Holy Spirit, suddenly I heard a loud scream as my friend dropped the phone and a spirit left her. I was stunned by this, and so was she.

It had never entered my mind that God would want to chat with us on the telephone. But just as I was coming to terms with the fact that He loves us so much He'll turn up anywhere to minister to our needs, He did it again. He interrupted another one of my phone calls. Laura phoned me, excited about a job interview she had been to. It was a wonderful job, assistant buyer for a major sports company. She had done extremely well in the interview and was desperately hoping she would be called for a second one.

As Laura was speaking, suddenly the Holy Spirit manifested His presence in a powerful way in the kitchen where I was standing, and began to give direction. He made it clear that she was to relinquish the job to Him, to either open or close the door as He, in His wisdom, saw fit. Laura was sad at hearing this, but she agreed and followed me in a prayer, releasing the situation to the Lord.

Several days later, Laura was offered the job. She was told there had been eight hundred applications for that one position. Even though she had little experience in this particular field, God had given the job to her. Everything God does is good.

I had read testimonies in books of God healing or fixing inanimate objects and thought it to be a fairly rare happening. About ten o'clock one night, I stood in our office at home sending a fax. My daughter, Angie, was using the computer and trying to print out notes for her university assignment. The printer would not work, however, and she had tried everything she knew to get it going. Angie is the technical "whiz" in the family, and if anyone could fix it, Angie could.

As I watched Angie pressing buttons and hitting the machine, suddenly God's presence filled the room. I looked at my daughter in astonishment. Neither of us was sick; we didn't need healing; so why had the Holy Spirit come in power? I decided that since power was flowing, it should be used to fix the printer so she could finish her assignment. All the furniture on the desk rattled as I laid hands on the equipment and commanded it to function in the name of Jesus. The printer began to work, Angie finished her assignment and we praised the Lord.

I left the room, but the anointing did not lift. I questioned the Lord as to why His presence was still upon me and asked Him what He wanted to do. "Go back into the study. I want to speak to Angie," was His reply. As I entered the study, the anointing increased and God told my daughter through a prophetic word that He had fixed the printer to demonstrate His love for her and to let her know that He is involved in both the big things and the small things in her life.

The Lord said to Angie that fixing the printer had been a small thing, but He knew she was concerned about bigger things, specifically getting a good job when she completed her business/law degree at the end of the year. Her grades were good, but not great, which meant competition would be tough, and the thought of not landing a good job after five years of study was causing her some stress. God told her He had it all in hand, and she was to trust Him for the outcome and not to worry.

A little later, as Anne, one of my intercessor friends,

prayed for Angie, God gave her a vision of an office building in Sydney. Sydney is the center of finance in our country, and Angie preferred to work there. My friend described seeing Sydney Harbor and described seeing Angie with a big smile on her face, standing in an office there. Not long after that, Angie was summoned to Sydney for a job interview with one of the top accounting firms in the world, one of the "big five." She was offered a job on the spot during the first interview.

As Angie sat staring out of the window that day at Sydney Harbor, she could not help but smile. It had happened just as God had shown. There had been fifty positions and a thousand applicants. Angie's university friends knew her grades, and they were all puzzled as to how she got the job ahead of so many other applicants. Truly, God is doing some amazing things at this point in time, and we are privileged to be part of them. There is most definitely a river flowing from God's throne, and it is getting deeper and wider.

I was very excited to be in a meeting a few months ago where I saw gold dust falling for the first time. The worship was particularly powerful that night, and as we glanced at the floor, we noticed it was sparkling. Gold dust covered the whole room. Fifty adults looked really funny crawling around on hands and knees, collecting that gold dust to take home. Now, gold dust continues to fall — sometimes a little, some-times a lot.

A couple of weeks later, I was in a church service where, for the first time, I saw people receive gold fillings in their teeth supernaturally during the ser-vice. What a night of excitement! God is revealing His glory in so many different ways.

Sarah recently announced to us she was quitting her job here in Brisbane and moving to Sydney be-cause she felt the job opportunities were better there. I was already trying to adjust to the idea of Angie's move to Sydney to take up her new job. In the mean-time, Laura had married and was living there too. My husband, Geoff, and I were beginning to wonder what we would do with ourselves: three daughters gone in one year, and all to another city.

Sarah's sudden decision jolted me; I had thought she would be at home for another year or so at least. I bought her a small gift, a delicate little bracelet, and we sat in the living room a couple of nights before she was to leave, talking and sharing. As I strapped the bracelet on her wrist, I lifted up her arm, and we were both shocked to discover both of her arms cov-ered in gold dust right up to her elbows.

Sarah and I stared at her hands for the next hour and a half, as large pieces of gold dust kept appear-ing. She collected as many pieces as she could pick up and wrapped them in a tissue. Finally, she went

off to bed ... only to come rushing downstairs shriek-
ing, "My suitcase and all the clothes I've packed are
covered in gold dust." We rushed upstairs and just
stood there staring, realizing that God was very much
in this move.

Since leaving for Sydney, Sarah and the other two
girls regularly find themselves covered with gold dust.
One of Sarah's friends, after seeing pieces of gold on
her shoulders, asked whether this meant the Second
Coming of Christ was near. Many are wondering!

Gold dust is appearing in the most unexpected
places, like in the car on the way home from worship
services, on a letter I posted to the mission field, on
sermon notes, Bibles, clothes — even on the dining
room table. Many times it seems to come for no apparent reason. One thing is for sure: it causes people
to ask questions. My hairdresser is, at present, devour-
ing books on God in response to this amazing
phenomenon. There is an evangelistic outworking of
this phenomenon. For those who are interested, Ruth
Ward Heflin, in her book *Golden Glory*, [4] discusses
this subject in some detail, giving many scripture ref-
erences regarding this phenomenon.

This anointing of gold dust and oil is transferable.
Recently, when visiting Robert and Anne, my brother-
in-law and sister-in-law, I asked if they had seen this
phenomenon in their church on the Central Coast.
They hadn't even heard of it. As I took my container

of gold dust out of my handbag to show them, Robert extended his arm and saw a large piece of gold on his wrist glistening under the light in the kitchen. At that moment, the presence of the Holy Spirit filled the room, and as I prayed for them, their hands began to glisten with gold dust. Anne fell to the floor under the power of the Spirit, having received a release in the gift of tongues. She lay on the kitchen tiles bathed in God's presence, while waves of peace flooded through Robert. For the next hour, well into the night, they sat and stared at their hands.

My prayer partners (Gail, Anne and Graeme) and I did the same thing when we first noticed gold dust and oil on our skin. We sat under a strong light for a long time staring at our hands, fascinated by this extraordinary phenomenon.

In this present move of the Spirit, God is linking some people together in teams so they can pray and minister together and support one another. I am not referring to friends who decide to form a prayer group, but rather to people whom God yokes together in the Spirit because He has a specific purpose for that unit. When it is the Holy Spirit doing the connecting, there is a great unity, and this becomes the group's strength against adversity. During the past two years, my three intercessor friends and myself have become aware that God was doing just such a work in the four of us.

The Holy Spirit would often give the four of us a piece of a jigsaw puzzle, and when we put the individual pieces together, we gained the required understanding. God sometimes wakes Anne in the middle of the night and gives her visions with warnings about Satan's strategies over various members of the four families represented. The Lord identifies particular family members by name so that we can intercede for them. The four members of the group all have different gifts, so that God will often show us all the same thing — in four different ways. When we minister together, we have what we call a "tag" ministry. The Holy Spirit comes upon one, then another, and we take turns as the anointing comes upon each of us.

Gail has begun to speak in languages she has not learned. Recently, she spoke in Korean and prophesied a healing ministry over a Korean couple. The couple did not speak English, and Gail does not understand Korean. The couple's daughter, who speaks both languages, translated the prophecy and confirmed that previous prophetic words had indicated the same thing. God has since taken Gail to Korea on a mission trip.

Graeme reports God moving powerfully on the streets of Brisbane among the homeless. Recent trips out on the "coffee van," with friends Russell and Betty (who do evangelistic work) saw some wonderful miracles. A woman asked for prayer, hoping that God would heal her asthma. As Graeme prayed for her, she leapt to her feet yelling, "I'm healed, I'm healed." God had healed her scoliosis as well. She ran off down the street to tell everyone.

A backslidden Christian woman came to the van for coffee, and through a word of knowledge, the Lord revealed to Graeme the woman's "miracle ministry." She had, indeed, ministered powerfully in the gift of miracles in the past, but because of hurt and rejection, she had left the church and was now living on the streets. Graeme was able to pray for her restoration that night.

Another man was led to the Lord, and wept as he confessed having bought a gun that day, intending to shoot himself the same night. God interrupted his plans. There is an increasing stream of people getting saved, healed and set free as God draws them to the "coffee van."

One night they had a very unusual miracle. They had all noticed, when they set out that day, that no one had remembered to buy tea bags and that there were only four tea bags in the box. They didn't think it would be a problem, because normally everyone they served asked for coffee. That night it was different. One after another asked for tea, and each time they reached into the box to get another bag and make another cup of tea, there was one left. After serving more than a dozen cups of tea, the team began to realize something unusual was occurring, and everyone became afraid to look in the box. Only a God who cares deeply for the homeless would show His love by multiplying tea bags.

This is all about God's love. This is about ordinary Christians being channels for the Holy Spirit, ordinary Christians taking Jesus to the world. The Lord will move through believers who are willing to set aside their own agendas and relinquish their own reputations, so that the love of Jesus can flow through them.

In Luke 10:27, Jesus gives us the great commandment to love the Lord our God with all our heart, soul, strength and mind, and our neighbor as ourselves. It is virtually impossible to truly love other people from the heart unless it is God's unconditional love flowing through us in the power of the Holy Spirit. In and of ourselves, we are too selfish.

When we are sold out to God and give ourselves as fully as we are able to Him — that is, to love Him with all our heart, soul, strength and mind — then it becomes possible to love our neighbor as ourselves because it will be His love in us. God's love is not the same as human sentimentality, which sometimes camouflages possessiveness and insecurity. God's love concerns itself with the very best welfare of those He loves.

Love involves action, for the Lord says that those who love Him obey Him (see 1 John 5:3). *"God is love"* (1 John 4:8); that is His nature, and He will only put His name to that which is born of love. This new move of God, which many are calling "an apostolic reformation," will see a return of the magnificent love of God, in His people and for His creation. God wants to perfect us in love and, in so doing, drive out fear. For *"the one who fears is not made perfect in love"* (1 John 4:18). God wants the Church to be a love letter from the Father to the world. Out of this love will come unity, and then we will be invincible against the enemy, as we stand together.

God is hearing the crescendo of petitions ascending to His throne, and He has promised to send the refreshing rain of His Spirit, if we turn to Him and seek Him:

> *"If my people, who are called by my name, will humble themselves and pray and seek my face and turn from their wicked ways, then will I hear from heaven and will forgive their sin and will heal their land."*   2 Chronicles 7:14

The early rain of revival has begun to fall, and, as a sign of it, droplets of water are literally falling on many believers while they are indoors.

There is a nearness to God that we can experience

when we commit ourselves wholeheartedly to seeking Him. We can learn about this from the descendants of Zadok. Zadok was high priest in the time of King David, and his descendants remained faithful to God in their tasks as priests, when other Levites had wandered off after idols, abandoning God and leading the people astray. In Ezekiel's vision of the Temple, the Zadokites, the faithful priests, were the only ones allowed to enter the sanctuary to minister to the Lord. They had kept God central in their lives; He was their only inheritance; He was their possession (see Ezekiel 44:28). Their reward for such consecration was the privilege of living in close proximity to the sanctuary of the Lord (see Ezekiel 48:9-12). They got to be closest to God's presence.

This is what we, the believer priests, are longing for — closeness to God. Those crying out for revival want to experience God's glory. That glory comes as we approach the Lord in holiness, in unity and in the power of His Spirit. Just as God would not allow the sacred anointing oil in the Tabernacle of Moses to touch any flesh (see Exodus 30:32), so He will not allow any flesh, in the form of human agendas, today. If we desire to flow with what God is doing and move under His anointing, carrying His glory, then we must be willing to do things His way.

This move of God is for everyone. Anyone willing to approach God on His terms can jump right into the river and start swimming. The Lord wants to make His abode with us ordinary people; He wants to lavish His love on us and show the world what a good God He is. He truly does! But it all begins with laying hold of Him. We must lay hold of Him for ourselves, because when we have His presence, we have everything. Nothing is more beautiful than the constant, close company of Jesus.

Simon experienced the excitement of God's manifest presence a few days after coming to know Jesus as his Savior, when oil oozed out of his fingertips. This young man had been hooked on drugs for years and had reached the stage of desperation when I met him. He was hungering to know a God who is real and who could change his life; he wanted help.

As I led Simon in the sinner's prayer, he experienced a mighty "whoosh" through his physical body, stronger than any ecstasy he had ever taken. A few days later, at a worship service, the oil coming out of his fingertips convinced him even more of the reality of his newfound Savior. Simon had jumped into the river of God with no agendas whatsoever and, as a result, was blessed with an experience of the tangible presence of the Holy Spirit. He then did what all new Christians do. He rushed to work the next day and told everyone he could find about how real Jesus is.

In this present apostolic move, God is blessing us and allowing us to physically experience His presence

— more so than in the past. For anyone who may be reading this and who has been longing for a greater experience of God's reality, be encouraged. The manifest presence of the Holy Spirit is not based on merit; it has to do with being open and with laying aside one's reputation. For any Christians who feel a bit dry and have perhaps lost their joy, a drink from the river of God will be greatly refreshing. A touch from the Master Himself will help them to refocus.

God has called us to focus on Him. As our whole lives are focused on worshiping Him, the constant experience of His tangible presence serves to remind us of the Great Commission. There are millions who long to know the one and only true God.

We worship, then work. That is the pattern shown us in the Tabernacle of Moses. There were no chairs to sit on in the Inner Chamber. The priests stood to eat the bread, fellowship and commune with God. There, in the sparsely furnished room, they would also refresh the oil, trim the wicks and burn fragrant incense. God's house is a place of worship and service, not entertainment and leisure. [5] We worship and get filled with the presence of the Holy Spirit, but then we take that presence and give it to others. This is God's plan for the Church.

Their life shall be like a watered garden, and all their sorrows shall be gone. The young girls will dance for joy, and men folk — old and young — will take their part in all the fun; for I will turn their mourning into joy and I will comfort them and make them rejoice, for their captivity with all its sorrows will be behind them.

Jeremiah 31:12-13, TLB

Eight

&

Cathy's Story

*N*ews on the church grape-
vine spreads fast. It wasn't
long before the phones started ringing. The message
was getting out that God had bestowed an unusual
healing gift on Cathy. Suddenly, she was experiencing x-ray vision. She could see straight through
people. As the Holy Spirit came upon her, she could
see the bones and internal organs and could point to
the trouble spots. Suddenly, invitations came in from
everywhere; everyone was intrigued by this new ability God had given Cathy. But let's back up a bit and
take a look at what led up to all this.

I met Cathy when she was referred to me by her
pastor for counseling. She had been diagnosed with
post traumatic stress disorder (PTSD), after being attacked in her own home by an intruder with a knife.
Cathy and her husband were doctors of natural

therapy and had been operating a clinic in the northern part of Queensland. After the assault, she and her husband moved to another town and left their profession, but they were still stalked incessantly. They moved further away, to Brisbane, but the stalking continued.

By the time I saw Cathy, she was a bundle of nerves. Not only was she feeling harassed and frightened, but her greatest concern was that she had almost completely lost her memory since the attack. She desperately needed to return to work for financial reasons, but without her memory, this was impossible. "Please help me get my memory back," she pleaded. "I can't do anything without it."

I asked Cathy to give me some background information regarding her family and childhood so I could gain a deeper understanding of factors that may have been influencing or contributing to her current condition. What unraveled was a heartbreaking tale.

Born in England in the late 1940s, to a nurse and a heart surgeon in an illicit affair, Cathy had been placed in an orphanage at birth. Her mother had died in childbirth, her biological father remained anonymous because of their secret affair, and her mother's husband rejected her, knowing she was not his.

Cathy remained in the orphanage until she was seven, when, she said, "a very fat lady and her husband" came and adopted her. Very shortly after this, the "fat lady" gave birth to her first child, a boy. It soon became evident that Cathy was there to care for the baby; she was free labor.

The painful memories of never being quite equal with her little brother brought tears to Cathy's eyes, as she described the deliberate, cruel treatment she received from her adoptive mother. If her brother was given a brand-new leather suitcase for school, Cathy would be given a small, cheap plastic one. If he was given a double ice cream cone, she would have one half the size. Not only did Cathy endure these insults throughout her childhood, but there were beatings and terror campaigns. Her mother would rip cotton sheets into thin strips and force Cathy to sew them back together by hand. When she had finished, her mother would rip them apart again. This was repeated over and over. Then there were the dead rats served up for dinner under a metal cover — just to taunt her.

Possibly the most fearful of all experiences, to Cathy, were the times she was sitting in the lounge room watching television, when the clock would lift off the wall all by itself, do a circuit of the room and set itself back on the hook. During those times and other times when furniture moved around unaided, Cathy sat motionless, too terrified to move. She would hear her mother in the bedroom nearby muttering and casting spells, as part of her witchcraft. If anyone in the household angered Cathy's mother, she would retreat to her room to gain revenge by calling upon the "spirits." One day, Cathy returned home from school to hear the neighbors warning of a naked lady running amok in the street. The police were called in to capture the woman, who turned out to be Cathy's mum.

These childhood stories culminated with Cathy fleeing from her mother, wedding dress in hand, trying to prevent any further damage to the gown. Her mother had been systematically ripping pieces off of it, in revenge and spite.

Cathy married and moved to Australia. The marriage did not last, but by the time Cathy was divorced, there were two children. Then, just a few years ago, Cathy had remarried and was now very happy with her second husband. Not long before, both of them had come to know Christ as Savior.

When I met Cathy, therefore, she already had this wonderful spiritual foundation. She had also been baptized in the Spirit, and God had raised her up as a powerful intercessor. He had healed her of a heart condition and of breast cancer. Although young in the Lord, this woman was making rapid progress and was hungry for as much of God as she could get. She was walking obediently with God and indicated a willingness to submit to the Lord in all things. Because of her openness to the Holy Spirit, Cathy was able to hear His voice very clearly and was learning to follow.

In our first counseling session, the Lord showed me the powerful spirit of rejection that had entered very early in Cathy's life, and which subsequently set the pattern for all the disasters which followed. She was ready to do whatever was necessary to be set free from the shackles of the past. She readily forgave those involved in contributing to her personal pain, and repented of wrong reactions or attitudes which had developed in her life.

As I broke the spirit of rejection off Cathy's life (through the power of the Holy Spirit), she felt something physically leave her body. She described to me a strange feeling she had experienced under her rib cage, somewhat like a flutter. It had been there as far back as she could remember, but now it was completely gone. She felt lighter; she felt different.

We prayed that the Lord would fill those empty places with His Holy Spirit and with peace. Cathy felt sleepy and relaxed, as the Lord's presence rested on her, and she was delighted in what He was doing.

When we got together for a second counseling session, the Lord brought to Cathy's memory more painful events that needed to be worked through, and the effects broken off her. As we prayed and asked the Holy Spirit to bring to the surface the things He wanted to deal with, Cathy suddenly remembered that, at the age of nine, she had visited her school teacher at home. When the teacher opened the garage door, the dead body of her father was hanging in front of them. This memory had been suppressed for more than forty years, but the Lord knew the damage it had done.

We prayed, asking the Lord for healing, and Cathy was gloriously set free. We also dealt with roots of bitterness that day, and the Lord reminded Cathy of the need to forgive her adoptive father for never having protected her from his wife's torment and abuse. He, too, had been moved by fear of her spiteful revenge and had retreated into silence.

It was necessary to break the power of witchcraft over this woman's life also. The Holy Spirit revealed that the physical attacks and constant stalking she had suffered recently stemmed from this influence in her life (even though Cathy had never been involved herself). We took the authority that is ours through the blood of Jesus Christ and prayed together, breaking the stronghold of the enemy. The stalking stopped from that time on.

Cathy's memory also returned. She reported, after the first session of ministry, a very rapid improvement and, after the second session, that her memory was virtually back to normal. God did a quick work, and in just two sessions, this client was free. Not all Christians who come for counseling have reached the point at which they are ready to cooperate with the Holy Spirit. Some only want relief from their symptoms and are not yet ready to make the changes needed for complete deliverance. Cathy was ready.

The devil had relentlessly tried to destroy Cathy from the time of her birth, and he was still "at it." He had gained an entry point early on through the rejection she had experienced, and that, in itself, had influenced Cathy's life from then on. She had been in spiritual bondage from circumstances beyond her control.

Bondages such as that suffered by Cathy can be easily and quickly broken by the power of the Holy Spirit, as He reveals to us the areas of specific need. This need not be a lengthy process. And, once this initial deliverance is accomplished, the emotional effects of the past usually settle over time, because now true healing can occur. The scab is no longer being picked off the sore again and again.

Cathy had exhibited physical symptoms from anxiety. These included memory loss, sleeping problems and general agitation. She had experienced emotions of fear, depression and intimidation. To attempt to treat all these symptoms without dealing with the spiritual roots would be a lengthy, time-consuming process, which might yield some measure of success depending on the skill of the counselor. If we can get to the root of the problem, and if that root is spiritual (as it often is), then the only way to remove it completely is by the power of God's Holy Spirit.

> *For though we live in the world, we do not wage war as the world does. The weapons we fight with are not the weapons of the world. On the contrary, they have divine power to demolish strongholds.*   2 Corinthians 10:3-4

Some problems are emotional, and some have a physical basis. Certainly, not all PTSD cases should be viewed as grounds for deliverance. We need wisdom and the Spirit's discernment.

While God is doing a quick work in this present move of His Spirit, most situations require more than two counseling sessions to bring resolution. Not everyone is as well prepared as Cathy was to receive healing, and doing the groundwork sometimes takes more time.

I mentioned the importance of God's timing in effecting a healing or deliverance of this kind, and nothing is more clear than God's timing for Cathy. When I saw Cathy the second time, she was feeling washed out and tired from being up all night. She described how she had gone to bed at the usual time feeling fine, only to wake suddenly in the early hours of the morning, shaking violently and feeling extremely hot. The shaking was so powerful it was disturbing her husband, who expressed some concern. This shaking continued for most of the night, and all the while, Cathy felt like she was on fire.

A few days later, Cathy was part of a prayer team at a miracle service and got the shock of her life. When a woman stood in front of her, she found she could see through the woman's body and watch her organs functioning. Having a background in naturopathy, Cathy is trained in anatomy and was able to name the various organs, nerves and arteries and to describe their condition. Then, a dog walked past, and Cathy shrieked, "Oh, no, I can see through the dog!"

There was general excitement all around. It soon became clear that the "fire of God" which had descended upon Cathy during the night was an impartation of the Holy Spirit, evidenced by the healing gift she began to flow in soon afterward. Satan attempted to destroy Cathy, but God reversed that damage and began using her life powerfully to give glory to His Name, to bless others and to fill her life with purpose. The ground the enemy had stolen was taken back.

Through the power of the Holy Spirit, this woman's life has been transformed from woundedness to being a powerful witness for Jesus Christ. Cathy has moved from defeat into victory and now stands as a testimony to the power of the blood of Jesus, to the finished work of the cross.

*For he has rescued us from the dominion of dark-
ness and brought us into the kingdom of the
Son he loves.*   Colossians 1:13

*But the people that do know their God shall be
strong, and do exploits.*   Daniel 11:32, KJV

Do not be anxious about anything, but in everything, by prayer and petition, with thanksgiving, present your requests to God. And the peace of God, which transcends all understanding, will guard your hearts and your minds in Christ Jesus.

Philippians 4:6-7

Nine

❧

Peace That Passes All Understanding

I was finishing up some sermon notes one day when the phone rang. Laura, in Sydney, had just come from her appointment with a head and neck surgeon, and she had been given some bad news. A small lump on the side of her face had been diagnosed as a tumor and would have to be removed as soon as possible. The doctor advised her that the lump, which was in her salivary gland, had reached a stage where it could become malignant at any time. If this occurred, he led her to believe, the cancer would rapidly spread to her brain, and she would have only a short time to live.

Removing the lump would require delicate surgery, as the salivary gland is close to facial nerves, and Laura was told that about ten percent of those who undergo this procedure are left with numbness in the facial area. This type of news is always extremely unsettling, and I found myself pacing the floor and claiming every scriptural promise I could think of regarding healing. For two hours, I walked the floor, feeling agitated and helpless. What made the news from the doctor even more foreboding was the fact that surgery could not be scheduled for another five weeks.

I had to stop praying and hurry off to the weekly Bible study with the men in a local homeless shelter. I was looking forward to the distraction, as I always came away encouraged by my time with "the guys," loving the honesty that met me there.

When I got back home, my mind returned to my most recent misery. I couldn't even share my anxiety, as my husband Geoff was overseas on a business trip and was still unaware of our daughter's diagnosis. As I pondered all the possibilities, the Lord began to speak to me. He told me to listen to my own preaching, and as my mind went back over the message I had just shared with those men, the Lord began to speak to me about my daughter and what He wanted to do in her life. A peace settled over me as I heard the Lord's voice. I was reassured, just to know He was involved. While I already knew that He was in the situation with us, it was His still small voice that comforted me.

The next day, reality hit. I was in the process of planning a mission trip and was due to leave in about two weeks. Laura's surgery was scheduled in the middle of the trip, but I would have to purchase my ticket soon. A quick decision needed to be made. I contacted the other two members of the team, Robyn and Judy, and asked them to pray with me that God would show me whether I was to go or remain with my daughter during her difficult time. As they quickly reminded me, if I did not go, neither could they. I was leading the team.

The trip had been planned for about eight months, and many sacrifices had been made for us to go. This latest news was discouraging and brought confusion to our plans. The Bible clearly tells us that the thief comes only to steal, to kill and to destroy, but that Jesus came to give us abundant life (see John 10:10). We all agreed that this was a spiritual battle and that we were being opposed by principalities and spiritual powers in high places, especially since we were going to a very religious nation which did not welcome the preaching of the Gospel.

We gathered together a large group of intercessors and sought God. Almost immediately, the answer came, and there was agreement all around that we were to go. The Lord spoke to me from several scripture passages:

> "*Anyone who loves his father or mother more than me is not worthy of me; anyone who loves his son or daughter more than me is not worthy*

> *of me; and anyone who does not take his cross*
> *and follow me is not worthy of me. Whoever finds*
> *his life will lose it, and whoever loses his life for*
> *my sake will find it."*   Matthew 10:37-39

> *"But seek first his kingdom and his righteous-*
> *ness, and all these things will be given to you as*
> *well."*   Matthew 6:33

Then the Lord reminded me of the time when Laura was born and of how He had met my need at that time. It had been a difficult birth, a Caesarean section, and I had been in the hospital for nine days, almost ready to go home, when I began to hemorrhage. I knew that if I did not stop bleeding, I would be sent back to the operating theatre. That prospect terrified me, since I'd had a bad experience with the anesthetic.

I pleaded with God to heal me so that I did not have to face the situation. All through the day and all through that night, I wrestled with God in prayer, while every half hour the nurses came in to check my vital signs.

I was beginning to feel desperate as the morning approached, knowing what awaited me. Then, at about five o'clock in the morning, the Lord spoke to me. He reminded me that He was Lord over all operating theatres, doctors and surgical procedures. He asked me, "Can't you trust Me?"

I repented of my lack of faith and made a decision to trust God to take care of me — even if it became necessary for me to have additional surgery. At that point, the bleeding stopped, and my vital signs returned to normal. The nurse came in to check me, as she had been doing every half hour, and phoned the doctor to report that all was well. Surgery had been scheduled for 7 AM, but at six that morning, word went out to cancel it.

As I recalled that difficult and frightening time, I knew the Lord was reassuring me that He is *the same yesterday, and today, and for ever*" (Hebrews 13:8, KJV). He reminded me of the story of Jesus asleep in the back of the boat while the storm raged around Him, and I sensed that He was telling me to lie down in the back of the boat, just as Jesus had done. Figuratively speaking, He was instructing me to go on the mission trip with an attitude of being asleep in the back of the boat. As I took care of His interests in another nation, He was promising to take care of my interests back home. While I had experienced the supernatural peace of God many times before while passing through trials, I sensed the Lord was wanting to take me deeper, to help me grasp this truth more profoundly. I agreed, and when I did, a most amazing peace flooded my whole being.

As the days passed, I found myself totally at peace with the whole situation. I searched for anxiety, but could find none. I was worried that I was not worried. I wondered if I was in denial. Each time the doctor's negative words came to mind, I would begin to get drunk in the Spirit, almost like I was going to laugh. I had so much joy and so much peace I was sure it had to be abnormal.

I got on with the business of organizing the mission trip and kept forgetting Laura had a serious problem to contend with. When friends and family called to ask how she was doing, my memory was jolted that in the natural all was not well. I was experiencing God's inoculation against fear. This was the sovereign hand of God causing me to be able to function in a supernatural way to contend with and overcome Satan's strategy to prevent God's work from going ahead. The supernatural peace had come the moment I surrendered to the Lord's wishes and chose to go His way, not mine, to put Him first before my emotional needs and my daughter's.

If this was the Lord's will for me, then I expected that He would grant Laura the capacity to release me willingly to go, and that became the test for me. She did. When I explained how I sensed God leading in this situation, she gladly released me to go, with no hesitation.

This was a time of testing for me and also a time of maturing for my daughter. God had never placed me in a situation like this before any other mission trip, despite the usual spiritual opposition that is experienced. This was also a good opportunity for Laura to learn to rely primarily upon her new husband for emotional support.

Laura had been planning to fly to Brisbane to spend a few days visiting friends and family before any of this happened. Since she already had her plane ticket, we agreed it would be good to arrange some healing ministry for her during her visit. Our church had recently been seeing some wonderful healings, some of them of serious illnesses like cancer. There was a sense of expectancy as I spoke with my pastor and made plans for Laura to attend a healing service.

We all knew that God could instantaneously dissolve the lump in Laura's salivary gland. This type of miracle had been witnessed before. In her case, however, it did not happen. She was prayed for, but God seemed intent on addressing other issues in her life first.

We all praised and thanked God, regardless of the fact that a miracle of healing did not occur. As I pondered the situation and reminded the Lord of how simple it would have been for Him to touch that tumor and have it disappear, He reminded me of how difficult it is to get a mother who desperately loves her child to experience total peace when the child faces a potentially deadly illness. "Isn't this the greater miracle?" I sensed Him say.

I had to agree, in my situation at least. For me to keep forgetting the doctor's grim prognostications and to be able to go about my day in total trust, knowing God had everything in hand, was the greatest miracle of all. I was asleep in the back of boat, and the storm was raging all around me. I do not believe I had ever experienced such deep and supernatural peace at this level before.

God's promise to us is that, as we look to Him, in the midst of difficult and frightening circumstances, as we focus on Him, trusting Him for the outcome, we will experience a supernatural peace (see Isaiah 26:3). This is not something we learn overnight. Rather, the Lord builds us up in our faith with each challenging situation we encounter. As we are healed and set free from emotional wounds and fears, we are able to trust more. As we learn how to take God at His word, relying on the goodness of His character to do what is best for us, the Holy Spirit will bring a beautiful peace. Peace is a fruit produced by the Holy Spirit as we abide in Christ and is part of our covenant blessings.

It was Jesus who first demonstrated this supernatural peace while in the midst of a terrible storm (see Matthew 8:23-27). The ironic thing is that as we let go, we receive it. Peace flows in as we relinquish our own desires and exchange them for the Lord's. Divine peace, God's supernatural provision, flows out of the security we experience in our Father, and it is available to all who belong to Him.

"But you will receive power when the Holy Spirit comes on you; and you will be my witnesses in Jerusalem, and in all Judea and Samaria, and to the ends of the earth."

Acts 1:8

Ten

🐚

To the Ends of the Earth

*B*efore Jesus ascended into Heaven, He told His disciples that the Holy Spirit would come upon them in power and that, as a result, they would spread throughout the whole earth as His witnesses (see Acts 1:8). The Lord was now taking us to what we considered to be *"the ends of the earth,"* to Nepal.

Robyn, Judy and I left on our mission trip as scheduled, despite great spiritual opposition, which left behind what looked like a trail of casualties. My family members were not the only ones in the line of fire. One of the other women on the team had experienced her elderly mother suddenly being admitted to the hospital for surgery two weeks before we were to leave.

Also prior to our leaving, one of the intercessors supporting us had a near accident in her car, and another had a head-on collision. Although his car was a total write-off, he escaped without a scratch.

These incidents with cars proved to be a solemn reminder of the importance of praying daily for protection. While we were away and traveling through mountains by car, we narrowly missed a head-on collision with a huge truck coming around a bend. The Lord had warned us what was coming when one of the women suddenly burst into tongues in the back of the car about three minutes before the incident. Intercessors pay a price for standing in the gap, and they bear the burden of those they pray for as a form of identification, just as Jesus did for us.

Several other intercessors became ill with upper respiratory infections and chest problems. Everyone was absolutely undaunted by the situations we found ourselves in, knowing that we were taking enemy ground and that the victory would not be gained without a fight.

When we arrived at our destination, we discovered that Samuel, the evangelist we would be traveling with, had been experiencing similar problems. His office had been broken into, with money and documents stolen. He had also been experiencing persecution of various kinds, including false accusations.

I do not report these events to highlight the enemy's activities, but rather to paint a realistic picture of what

we can expect to experience when we attempt anything for God, particularly the evangelization of
non-Christian nations. Also, to attempt to encourage
the believers in such nations will attract strong opposition, as the devil works hard to keep them
discouraged, so they will have difficulty rising up and
winning their own people to Christ.

Samuel was extremely glad to see us and shared
for many hours his heart for the tribal people of his
country. He works with the underground church,
moving among all the different denominations, and
is a "hidden one," as he likes to put it, in his nation.
Many times, he has been beaten for his faith. He bears
the scars on his head where he was attacked and then
left for dead. Samuel is willing to die for his faith.
He, like other evangelists in his land, has been ar-
rested and harassed by police and politicians. All this
meant that we were in for an interesting time.

We set off the day after we arrived for the villages,
where we were to hold a women's conference and
minister in several churches. In the back of the car
on the way, the three of us found our clothes covered in gold and silver dust. This happened every day
throughout the trip, a continual reminder of God's
presence and glory. Because we were in remote areas,
where tourists are not often seen, people walk long
distances to attend functions that are held. They are

excited to see visitors, just as we were excited to meet them and hear what God was doing among their people.

We soon got accustomed to the goats, the cows and the chickens, as we tramped through vegetable gardens and fields of crops to get to the little church buildings or, in some cases, to mud huts. It was always a joy to see the Christians waiting for us with big smiles on their faces and bowing to us with the customary Christian greeting, which we soon learned in the native language. It was wonderful to join with these brothers and sisters on the other side of the world and worship the Lord together.

God was faithful, and the Holy Spirit came in power in every meeting to minister to the people. We rejoiced to see many healed each time we prayed. The Lord had laid upon our hearts to teach and preach on the victory of the cross, so for almost two weeks we shared strong faith messages, along with personal testimonies, encouraging the believers to reach out for all that is ours through Christ, refusing to be robbed by the enemy.

We bid farewell to the tribal people in that area and made our way over the mountains to another district, where we were scheduled to teach for several days in a Bible school which Samuel had begun several years earlier. There were seven students in the school when we arrived, ranging in age from sixteen to nearly fifty. A couple of them had already been pastoring village churches, but wanted to receive some formal training. Most of the others were young men who desired to become evangelists. They would go back into the mountainous regions where their tribes lived. We found them all to be keen students, anxious to learn as much as possible. The principal of the school was an excellent translator for us and made communicating relatively easy during our time in the classroom.

As we were finishing up our time of teaching, Samuel announced that he had been able to organize another women's conference. He thought this would be an excellent opportunity for all the women in the surrounding districts to come together and be encouraged. He informed us that we were to hold the conference the next day from 9 AM to 4 PM. He expected about a hundred women to be coming.

This came as a surprise, as we thought we had finished our time of ministry. Robyn, Judy and I had been invited out for dinner that evening and were sure we would not get back to the hotel in time to put together seven hours of teaching material. We all felt a bit panicky, but the Lord had been very gracious to us thus far.

I had phoned home and discovered that Laura had come through her surgery well and had been given a good report. The meetings were going well, and God's hand could clearly be seen in everything that we were doing. But now, we were faced with quite a challenge.

The three of us returned to our hotel at about 9:30 that night, not long before our usual bedtime. Robyn and Judy sat on the ends of their beds staring at me. "What do we do now?" they asked.

I began to pace the floor, asking God for His strategy for the next day. They, too, prayed. How could we possibly run a conference for a hundred women for seven hours with no time to prepare? We really needed to hear from God!

Suddenly, God's presence filled the room. As the Holy Spirit began to speak to me, I could hardly believe what I was hearing. Surely not! But then I shared with the others what I felt God was saying, and they agreed that is the way the Lord works.

The Holy Spirit had said to me something along these lines: "For the past two weeks, you have been preaching faith messages, telling the people that the Christian life must be lived by faith in the power of the Holy Spirit. You have been telling them they must put aside all human agendas and be willing to follow only My agenda for their lives, and intimating that they may lose their reputations along the way. You have been telling them they must learn to hear the voice of the Holy Spirit so they can take their places in the Body of Christ and fulfill their callings. Now, you are going to demonstrate all that teaching in one day; you are going to show them how it is done."

The Lord told us not to prepare a plan for the following day, but to stand up before the people, listen to His voice and do only what He told us to do. He assured us that He would guide us throughout the day. He wanted His people to have fresh manna, not stale food. He wanted the wind of His Spirit to blow upon His people to refresh and revitalize them, as many were discouraged and weary, burdened with many cares. He wanted to lift them up on eagles' wings and give them His joy to strengthen them.

I felt like I was being asked to walk on water. Before I had left on the trip, I sensed I was to lie down in the back of the boat. But now I was being asked to step out of the boat. I was learning that faith can be expressed in both inactivity and activity, depending on what the Holy Spirit is saying to do at the time. To do the wrong one at the wrong time is the opposite to faith. And only when faith is exercised will the arm of God be moved.

I had been placed in this uncomfortable position by the Lord before, only not for such an extended period of time. I could see how He had been building up to this, as the previous mission trip to Zambia six months earlier had been a real testing time for me. I had arrived in Johannesburg, South Africa, the first night of the trip. At about 4 AM, I found myself wide awake, owing to jet lag. No sooner had I opened my eyes than I heard the Lord tell me that on this particular trip He was going to teach me to function in the power of the Spirit, with no warning at all and no preparation. I thought the Lord was referring to preaching, especially in crusades, and thought this lesson might be interesting.

It turned out to be interesting all right. God had not only meant that I would function in the power of the Spirit in preaching. He had meant it in a much greater sense, in most everything a Christian does in relation to ministry. Over and over again, I was called upon with no warning, sometimes in front of large groups of people. All of this practice was most helpful now that we were faced with doing a whole day's conference by faith.

We watched the women arriving in their brightly colored costumes, some with babies on their backs, some with their elderly mothers in tow. Many had walked for several hours down from the mountains and across the river to get to the meeting. Many were pregnant. Robyn, Judy and I were all feeling a mixture of fear and excitement, waiting to see what God was going to do. We were rather pleased that not quite one hundred came, owing to some miscommunication, and also a little relieved that the conference started late, as women were still traveling to get there.

Finally, the time arrived, and I stepped to the front

to address the crowd. I was trusting that when I opened my mouth God would fill it, because He said He would. And He did. The Lord first spoke to us through a prophetic word about the river which was flowing rapidly past the building we were in and which could be seen from the window. He talked about rivers of living water flowing from within us, and pointed to the fact that a river is never static; it keeps moving and changing shape. In order to keep moving, we have to pay attention; that will cost us our time and maybe our reputations.

The Lord was, indeed, faithful to His word and came and led us throughout the day. God graciously healed several women miraculously, and much to our surprise and delight, three women got saved. We were surprised because we had been told all the women coming would be Christians. Then God gave us another delightful surprise. Towards the end of the meeting, as we glanced at the floor, we saw gold dust all over the area where we had been praying for the sick. This had been the first time I felt led to talk about the gold dust in that country, and I had done it at the beginning of the meeting. Now, Samuel, the principal of the Bible school and others gathered around to see the glory of God displayed. The women were excited with what God had been doing throughout the day and were gratefully praising Him for encouraging and refreshing them.

Until we had told Samuel about the gold dust and oil, he had neither seen it nor heard about it. After all, there were no Christian book shops and little access to the Internet in the remote areas of that country. In all of Samuel's travels around the country, evangelizing and encouraging the churches, he had not seen the gold dust. So we were especially excited, realizing that it might be a totally new experience to that land.

The next night, as we sat eating dinner, I spotted a brilliant green piece of glittery material on Samuel's face, on his cheekbone. As the light shone on him, it sparkled brightly. The other two women jumped up to come and see, and as we all examined his face, we also noticed the shoulders of his jacket were covered with silver pieces larger than the normal dust. When he lifted his hands, there was a circle of gold dust in his right palm. We all rejoiced that God's glory was all over this young evangelist, who could now take the anointing and spread it throughout the country, as he goes from village to village and from town to city, preaching the Gospel of Jesus Christ. He now had a new sign following his preaching that would make many people wonder.

The next morning we had our last church meeting in the city, where a young woman pastor had recently been led of God to plant a new congregation. Samuel later told us that this fiery young preacher had an unusual and powerful testimony. She had prayed the

sinner's prayer in a hospital just before she was expected to die. The doctors pronounced her dead, and
for several days she lay in the hospital, apparently
dead. A group of Christians came and took her body
away and prayed life into her. She was thus raised
from the dead, and is now becoming a powerful
Christian leader in that nation. She also had not seen
nor heard of the gold dust. As we shared about what
God is doing around the world, the gold dust fell
again all over the floor where we had been seated.

The last couple of days before we left to return
home were days of reflection. We were able to discuss what the Lord had done and what we had
learned. In what way were we returning home different? It was during this time that I had a dream
that I felt was significant and that I believe was from
the Lord.

In the dream, I could see a staircase. The steps were
wide and gently graduated. At the top of the staircase
and to the side, was a wall that was broken. There
was a gap, or breach, in the wall, and many Christians were jumping off a steep embankment through
this gap in the wall in order to reach their destinations more quickly. They were not willing to take the
safer way down the steps because they considered it
too slow and did not understand the importance of
gradual progression. There were many wounded
people at the bottom. Some had twisted ankles or

broken legs, and one man appeared to be paralyzed with a broken back. It was such a distressing scene of unnecessary injury and devastation that I went and found the senior pastor of these Christians and implored him to close the gap in the wall to prevent further injury to the people. He was the one who had the authority to rebuild the wall.

When I asked the Lord the meaning of the dream, I came to some understanding. Steps are symbolic of our spiritual progress or Christian walk, [1] and walls are symbolic of protection or separation. [2] I was reminded of the story of Joseph and his preparation for service to God. Joseph was led by God step-by-step through the trials of his faith until God was satisfied the young man was equipped for the task ahead and ready to handle promotion. Then God released Joseph with a powerful anointing to accomplish the task he had been given. Because Joseph was released in God's perfect timing, he was mature and able to be a blessing to many, as he was placed in leadership.

I felt the dream was speaking of the way the enemy entices Christians to run ahead of God, moving into places of ministry and influence prematurely, unaware of the danger of quick promotion. Adequate time must be given to allow the Lord to build a firm foundation, to test its strength and then erect a strong structure upon it. Otherwise, there is lack of wisdom, knowledge yet unattained and healing not yet received. The Holy Spirit's power to change lives has not yet been imparted.

The kind of wounding experienced by those released ahead of God's timing can take years to heal, and some never fully recover — all because of the enemy's lies. For Eve, when the fruit from the tree of the knowledge of good and evil seemed appealing, the end result was destruction. Learning restraint is part of the maturing process. The inability to delay immediate gratification reveals our immaturity to ourselves and to others.

In the dream, those who chose the steady, but slower, path to their destinations arrived safely and in a relaxed, unstressed condition. These were ready to take up the next challenge; they were in the right place at the right time.

I asked the Lord why the staircase was going downward in the dream and not upward, which would seem to indicate promotion. My understanding of this is that the way to be elevated in spiritual things is to take the downward path, as far as self is concerned. As we decrease, God can increase, and in due time He will raise us up. Humility comes before honor (see Proverbs 15:33). Many are saying that the Lord is speeding up the time taken to mature in spiritual things, and while that may be the case, the process remains the same. Our faith still must be tested. There is preparation time for all of us.

God has told us to go and preach the good news to all creation with signs and wonders following (see Mark 16:15-18). Witnesses do more than talk about Jesus; they demonstrate His life. We are to be *as* Jesus to the world. The passion and anointing to obey the Lord's command flows directly from our relationship with Him. Our intimacy with Him in the prayer closet determines the doors of opportunity for service that God will open. But the Lord does not call us to a specific work as such. Rather, God calls us to Himself, for service only ever flows out of relationship. So we must first develop our relationship with the Lord. We need to lay hold of Him!

Many suggest that those who are intimate with the Bridegroom become a prophetic womb to bring forth His manifest presence in the earth. The world hungers for the presence of God, but very few know how to find it. Of those who do know how to find it, many are not willing to spend the time or pay the price to be imbued with Him. We, as believers in Jesus Christ, have the unique privilege and responsibility to go forth, taking the presence of Jesus to a lost world. But first we must tarry, spending precious preparation time, listening for the voice of the Holy Spirit, just like the one hundred and twenty in the upper room ten days before Pentecost, and just like Simeon and Anna waiting for the coming Savior.

Service to God is all about being in the right place at the right time, understanding the seasons of God. It's about hearing His voice and following, yielding to the Holy Spirit again and again, until a beautiful, fragrant perfume emanates from our lives, a *Sweet Aroma* to our God. When we live like that, doors of opportunity for sharing the Gospel message will swing open before us. Whether we are witnesses for Jesus in our own nation or in foreign lands does not matter. What matters is our passion for Jesus revealed in our obedience. This blesses the heart of God.

But thanks be to God! For through what Christ has done, he has triumphed over us so that now wherever we go he uses us to tell others about the Lord and to spread the Gospel like a sweet perfume. As far as God is concerned there is a sweet, wholesome fragrance in our lives. It is the fragrance of Christ within us, an aroma to both the saved and the unsaved all around us. To those who are not being saved, we seem a fearful smell of death and doom, while to those who know Christ we are a life-giving perfume.

2 Corinthians 2:14-16, TLB

Eleven

The Fragrance of Jesus

Without Jesus, we have the stench of death over our lives. Without Him, we have no hope, just the ongoing drudgery of being weighed down by the cares of life. But we don't have to carry our own burdens when we know the Lord, because He took them all to the cross. He died for our sins, our sicknesses and our sorrows. This incomprehensible gift is given to us by God the Father, whose grace and love flow out to us like a mighty river. This river of love washes over us, cleansing, healing and restoring us through the blood of His Son. We have been liberated by the supreme sacrifice of Christ our Savior. Sin and death have no hold over us.

Young Tim discovered this. He had been a Christian for four days when I met him. Twice during that time, God had pinned him to the floor. The first time, he was baptized in the Holy Spirit. The second time, his malignant brain tumor was healed.

Tim was all of about eighteen years old, and his life had been a living hell up until this time. Diagnosed with attention deficit hyperactivity disorder and epilepsy, among other things, Tim had almost destroyed himself with drugs and alcohol. He had been to the hospital for his regular checkup two days before, and the doctors could not find the brain tumor. The scan showed his brain clear, as if a tumor had never been there. The doctors had previously said that Tim would not live to see the year out. They were so puzzled they did not know what to do and hurried him out of the hospital in bewilderment.

Tim was singing God's praises at the homeless shelter. Like the other guys there, he readily admits that the reason he had been homeless was either drugs, alcohol, gambling or "all of the above." But now he was jumping with joy and was busy trying to convince another young fellow that alcohol didn't do anywhere near as good a job of blotting out the pain of reality as Jesus did. The other young fellow wasn't so convinced. I could overhear him saying, "But alcohol's so easy; it just blots out everything."

"No, mate, you've gotta give your life to Jesus."

So went the conversation.

Without Jesus, we have nothing, and without Him, we are nothing. Without Jesus there is no *Sweet Aroma*, just a stench. Jesus is the fragrance of our lives. This beautiful fragrance that He emits was foreshadowed thousands of years ago in the Tabernacle of Moses.

The golden Altar of Incense in the Holy Place not only speaks to us of the prayers and intercession of the saints, but it also signifies Christ in His ministry of prayer and the intercession of the Holy Spirit in the Church. It is also meaningful that the Altar of Incense was at the very heart of the Tabernacle, indicating that the ministry of intercession, prayer and praise are at the very heart of God. The fire on this altar was lit by God Himself, indicating that it is the fire of the Holy Spirit, which causes the fragrance to rise. God only accepts incense that He Himself has prescribed; there was to be no strange, or foreign, fire or incense upon this golden altar. God will not accept imitations. [1]

The special-formula incense, or sacred perfume, which God instructed Moses to make and burn upon the altar, was symbolic of the belief in and confession of the presence of Yahweh in the midst of Israel. The ingredients were rare and costly, indicating that only the best is to be employed in the worship of God. [2] Indeed, the ingredients of the incense speak to us of the qualities the Lord desires in our lives, those characteristics that please Him and that give off a fragrant aroma:

> And the LORD said to Moses, "Take sweet spices, stacte, onycha and galbanum, and pure frank-

> *incense with these sweet spices; there shall be*
> *equal amounts of each. You shall make of these*
> *an incense, a compound according to the art of*
> *the perfumer, salted, pure and holy. And you*
> *shall beat some of it very fine, and put some of*
> *it before the Testimony in the tabernacle of meet-*
> *ing where I will meet with you. It shall be most*
> *holy to you. But as for the incense which you*
> *shall make, you shall not make any for your-*
> *selves, according to its composition. It shall be*
> *to you holy for the* LORD*. Whoever makes any*
> *like it, to smell it, he shall be cut off from his*
> *people.*   Exodus 30:34-37, NKJ

Stacte was a fragrant sap, or gum, from a beautiful perfumed shrub, and the word means "that which drips." It is a fragrant kind of myrrh that flows spontaneously out of the bark of the tree when it splits naturally. As the sap dries, it forms clumps known as "tears." To me, this is reminiscent of the free-flowing tears of intercession. A beautiful anointing will flow from our lives when we stay in step with the Holy Spirit:

> *Whoever believes in me, as the Scripture has*
> *said, streams of living water will flow from*
> *within him.*   John 7:38

Stacte, in its pure form, is rare and very valuable. [3]

Onycha was a substance extracted from a shellfish taken from the Red Sea. It derived its fragrance from the things it fed on. Onycha means "to roar" or "to groan," and speaks to us of the anointing flowing out of the depths of our beings as we feed upon the things of God. God wants our worship to come from deep within our innermost beings:

> In the same way, the Spirit helps us in our weakness. We do not know what we ought to pray for, but the Spirit himself intercedes for us with groans that words cannot express.
>
> Romans 8:26

Galbanum was a gummy, resinous juice from a tree-like plant growing in Syria, Persia and Africa. When any part of the plant was broken, the juice, or sap, would flow from a tough, fatty substance of strong, piercing smell and sharp, warm taste. [4]

Lori Wilke, in her book *The Costly Anointing*, beautifully describes the symbolism she sees in this substance. She points out that galbanum means "fatty" or "rich" and that those who carry a rich, heavy anointing are people who have been broken and tempered by the Holy Spirit. [5]

> The sacrifices of God are a broken spirit; a broken and a contrite heart, O God, you will not despise.
>
> Psalm 51:17

The Scriptures tell us that Jesus learned obedience from the things He suffered (see Hebrews 5:8). We also must be broken before God can use us:

> *During the days of Jesus' life on earth, he of-*
> *fered up prayers and petitions with loud cries*
> *and tears to the one who could save him from*
> *death, and he was heard because of his reverent*
> *submission.*   Hebrews 5:7

Frankincense was considered a precious perfume. It comes from the sap of a tree and is white in color. It was one of the gifts given to the baby Jesus by the wise men and also one of the burial spices, and it represents the high priestly ministry of Christ as He lives to intercede for us. The white color speaks to us of purity and righteousness.

> *I will go the mountain of myrrh and to the hill*
> *of incense. All beautiful you are, my darling;*
> *there is no flaw in you.* Song of Songs 4:6-7

The anointing that flows from our lives will be directly related to our prayer lives and our submission to the Lord in obedience.

Salt was added to the sacred incense as a seasoning and a preservative, and also as a symbol of purification. Jesus said, *"You are the salt of the earth"* (Matthew 5:13). Salt speaks to us of pure and gracious speech. [6]

> *Let your conversation be always full of grace,*
> *seasoned with salt, so that you may know how*
> *to answer everyone.*   Colossians 4:6

All of the spices, the sweet and bitter together, were crushed very fine, blended together with the frankincense and then tempered with salt. There were five ingredients, and there was a balance in all the ingredients, as they were of equal weight. Each ingredient was important to God and seen as necessary in order for the beautiful perfume to arise from the golden altar and permeate the whole sanctuary.

Jesus Christ was crushed, beaten and humiliated through His trials and sufferings, but His life came forth as a sweet perfume to the Father. As we identify with Jesus and enter into His sufferings, the self-life will be crushed out of us, and we will become permeated with the fragrance of the Lord. As we minister to our Father in prayer and praise, surrendering our lives in obedience to the Holy Spirit, we prepare the way for the Lord's Second Coming, and He prepares us to take up our positions in the end-time army.

Most of us have times in our lives when we wonder what our positions are. We wonder if God can, or ever will, use us to impact this world. We look at our imperfections, our inadequacies, and it seems quite impossible for us to do something important. Some people never even stop to consider that God may have a calling on their lives; their limited thinking does not allow it. But when we cling to a perspective like that, we are actually seeing God as limited. We are believing that God is not big enough or able to do something useful with an imperfect person. If God made the whole universe out of nothing, then He is quite capable of taking you or me and doing something creative with us. He knows the gift He has placed within each one of us, and He knows how to draw it out so that we might be a blessing — to Him and to others.

I am still amazed that God used an African man on death row in a maximum security prison to bless and encourage me. Three years ago, I got a call from the editor of a Christian magazine in Adelaide, telling me their office had received a letter for me from a prisoner in Zambia. Apparently, a short story I'd written had found its way to Africa and ended up in the hands of a prisoner on death row. The man was a Christian, and he wrote to encourage me and let me know he was praying that I would be successful in the work the Lord had called me to do. I was touched that this man would bother to write and also very encouraged that he was so lifted up by his faith in the midst of his trials. Here is a brief excerpt from his letter. Although his name has been changed, I left the letter as he wrote it:

Dear sister in Christ Jesus, Elizabeth,

I firstly wish to send my warm greetings to you in the good name of the Lord Jesus. My name is Matthew, writting from the above addressed prison of Zambia in africa. I am aged 40. I am serving a death sentence at the same prison. Nevertheless paul the apostle said, "Therefore there is now no condemnation to him in Christ Jesus" *(Romans 8:1). Truly these are very encouraging words to a suffering soul like me, as far as the situation I am in is concerned. This makes my faith in the Lord Jesus not fail always. …*
I write with joy after having heard about your faith in Christ Jesus in these hard and difficult times in this world. But the apostle paul truly said, "our citizenship is in heaven" *(philippians 3:20), so, we know that all the problems and all the Loneliness are only for a short time.*

The last time I wrote to Matthew, he did not respond. Perhaps he has left this world. He proved to me that it doesn't matter who we are or where we are; obedience to Jesus always releases a fragrance from our lives.

A man just released from prison wandered up to us at the coffee van recently, weeping, afraid that he could not cope with the life he faced. He had been on the streets for three days, sleeping under bridges at night. His clothes were getting dirty, and he felt very ashamed. We sat on the pavement and listened while he told us what a total failure he was. He had completely messed up his life.

His mother and father had both raped him as a child. His father had grabbed his genitals and crushed them so that he was unable to father children himself. He had murdered his father, slit his throat. For this, he served fifteen years in jail. He now had an alcohol problem and could not earn a living following a motorcycle accident. The man sobbed as I explained that he was not only a victim once, but twice. He was living as a victim, continually being punished because he was still holding all the pain and bitterness inside.

"How can I possibly forgive them for what they did to me?" he sobbed.

"You can make a mental choice to forgive," I explained, "and ask God to help you with the rest. You can say, 'I choose to forgive.' "

"I can do that," he sobbed.

We led him in a prayer of forgiveness for all the

cruelty experienced at the hands of his parents, and then we led him in a prayer of rededication to the Lord (he had been saved at fourteen, but had wandered away). The Holy Spirit descended upon the man right there on the street and lifted him up into His presence. With his face turned toward Heaven and his hands uplifted, he smiled, praised God and now wept tears of joy and thankfulness for burdens lifted and hope renewed. Others might give up on us, but God never does.

When I was a child growing up in the 1950s and 60s in Sydney, I would sometimes go into the city shopping with my parents. On many occasions, as I walked through the busy streets, I would see written with white chalk on the pavement, in the most exquisite handwriting, the word *Eternity*. I saw it time and time again in different locations, and each time I saw it, I wondered what it meant and why eternity was so important to the person who was motivated to keep drawing attention to this inevitable reality.

Many years later, I read the testimony of Arthur Stace. He had been a derelict alcoholic, but that didn't stop God. He looked straight past Arthur's hopeless condition and reached down, saved his soul and changed his life.

Arthur had been born into poverty and became a ward of the state at twelve. He grew up to be a drunkard and petty thief who, after serving in France in

World War I, fell into drunken dereliction. He turned up at a Wednesday night men's meeting at a church in Sydney in August 1930, primarily to get a bun and a hot cup of tea. But Arthur got more than supper that night. After hearing the message of salvation, he knelt down under the bushes in the park across the road and gave his life to Christ. [7] In that moment, the drunkard was eternally changed.

Although Arthur could not write and could barely sign his own name, he learned to write the word *Eternity*, and soon began to write it in chalk on footpaths all over the city in beautiful script. For the next thirty-five years (he was unknown for the first twenty-five of them), he posed a searching, probing question to puzzled Sydneysiders — a one-word sermon. Until his death in 1967, at the age of eighty-three, Arthur Stace worked as an urban missionary influencing many for the Kingdom of God.

Only a gracious, merciful, creative God could take what society deems worthless and raise it up with dignity and hope. Just as Arthur Stace honored God, God has also honored Arthur. Over the Sydney harbor bridge, at the Millennium 2000 fireworks display, was written the word *Eternity* in memory of him, for all the world to see. The unwashed derelict from the park had become a fragrant aroma in the nostrils of Almighty God.

The life of Arthur Stace stands as testimony to the power of the unconditional love of our gracious God to heal the brokenhearted and the downtrodden. Satan's lies were exposed. Like countless multitudes before him, Arthur had accepted the spoken and unspoken messages that he was "no good" and that life is "hopeless" and so acted out his sense of insignificance through a derelict, alcoholic lifestyle. Just like the prostitute who sells herself on the street corner, the drug addict who shoots up in the alley, or the foodaholic who binges and purges, so also the alcoholic reflects his own self-hatred and hopelessness in the way he treats himself. Like everyone else, Arthur had a story to tell.

But God has demonstrated His love by sending His Son to die for us. God gave His firstfruits, His best gift, His Son, so that we might have eternal life. This speaks to us of our worth, our great value to God.

> *And God was pleased, for Christ's love for you was like sweet perfume to him.*
>
> Ephesians 5:2, TLB

> *Therefore, since we are surrounded by such a great cloud of witnesses, let us throw off everything that hinders and the sin that so easily entangles, and let us run with perseverance the*

race marked out for us. Let us fix our eyes on
Jesus, the author and perfecter of our faith, who
for the joy set before him endured the cross,
scorning its shame, and sat down at the right
hand of the throne of God.   Hebrews 12:1-2

The LORD was not in the wind. After the wind there was an earthquake, but the LORD was not in the earthquake. After the earthquake came a fire, but the LORD was not in the fire. And after the fire came a gentle whisper.

1 Kings 19:11-12

Twelve

The Church in Transition

There is a sense of expectancy in the Church, as we wait to see what God is going to do next. We know that changes are coming and that whenever the Lord does something new to build His Church, He provides new wineskins. For Jesus said:

> *"Neither do men pour new wine into old wineskins. If they do, the skins will burst, the wine will run out and the wineskins will be ruined. No, they pour new wine into new wineskins, and both are preserved."*   Matthew 9:17

Old structures must give way to new.

In order to gain a better understanding of these things, it helps to have some idea of the way in which God does things and where we are on God's calendar of restoration. The book of Acts describes an early

Church marked by power and rapid growth and influenced strongly by the first apostles. However, after the death of the early apostles, the Church gradually lost its cutting edge and lapsed into the Dark Ages for a thousand years.

Around 1500 AD the Lord began a restoration movement when Martin Luther began to teach "justification by faith." The Protestant Reformation was thus ushered in.

Since the time of Luther, there have been four major restoration movements: Protestant, Holiness/Evangelical, Classical Pentecostal and the Latter Rain/Charismatic. There were smaller movements of the Holy Spirit in between, and each time God has restored foundational biblical truths.

Dr. Bill Hamon points out, in his book *Prophets and the Prophetic Movement,* [1] that in the latter half of the twentieth century, God began to bring a fresh emphasis upon the fivefold ministry. He sees that from the 1950s onward, each decade saw a move of the Holy Spirit which focused afresh upon the roles of the evangelist, pastor, teacher, prophet and, more recently, the apostle.

Dr. Peter Wagner, a leading church growth scholar, is of the opinion that this present move of the Spirit is a work of God that is "changing the shape of Protestant Christianity around the world." [2] No longer are churches content to function within traditional denominational structures, but Dr. Wagner sees radical changes in such areas as local church government, worship styles, leadership training, evangelism, financing, missions, prayer and so forth. He has coined the term "The New Apostolic Reformation" to describe these sweeping changes which are occurring. The word *apostolic* is used in recognition of the present-day apostolic ministries and because it denotes a strong focus on outreach. [3] Previous movements have called themselves apostolic; hence the word *new*.

In his article "The Rise and Rise of the Apostles," Phil Marshall points out that we are at present witnessing the rise of the apostle in the worldwide Church. He goes on to say that this gift will play a crucial role in the missionary expansion of the Church this century. [4] This is because the Church is *"built on the foundation of the apostles and prophets with Christ himself as the chief cornerstone"* (Ephesians 2:20).

One of the chief prophetic voices in the Church today, Dr. Bill Hamon, argues that while full restoration of the gift of apostles is essential for the Church to come to maturity, apostolic ministry encompasses a broader dimension than just apostles. He believes that both ministers and church members will be used by God to perform signs, wonders and miracles. [5] God wants to send us all out into the community to be "as Jesus"!

The Bible tells us:

> *It was he who gave some to be apostles, some to be prophets, some to be evangelists, and some to be pastors and teachers, to prepare God's people for works of service, so that the body of Christ may be built up.*
> *From him the whole body, joined and held together by every supporting ligament, grows and builds itself up in love, as each part does its work.*
>   Ephesians 4:11-12 and 16

As I have pondered what the Church leaders are saying about the Church structure of the future, I have come to realize that before we can understand what God will do, we must first understand His heart. From Moses' words, as he instructed the Israelites, we get an idea of God's priorities:

> *These are the commands, decrees and laws the LORD your God directed me to teach you to observe in the land that you are crossing the Jordan to possess, so that you, your children and their children after them may fear the LORD your God as long as you live by keeping all his decrees and commands that I give you, and so that you may enjoy long life. ... Hear, O Israel: The Lord our God, the LORD is one. Love the LORD your*

God with all your heart and with all your soul
and with all your strength.
                              Deuteronomy 6:1-2 and 4-5

This passage links the fear of God, enjoying a long life and loving God with all our might. In Luke 10:27, Jesus confirms that we are to love God with all our heart, soul, strength and mind, and love our neighbor as ourselves. In Galatians 5:14, Paul tells us that the entire Law is summed up in a single command: *"Love your neighbor as yourself."* In the book of Romans, Paul tells us that love is the ful-fillment of the Law (see Romans 13:10). Anything to do with God will be marked by love because *"God is love"* (1 John 4:8).

As I pondered the issues involved in this apostolic move and the new apostolic leadership, I sensed the Lord saying that the central theme for everything He does in the days ahead will be Luke 10:27:

" 'Love the Lord your God with all your heart
and with all your soul and with all your strength
and with all your mind'; and, 'Love your neigh-
bor as yourself.' "   Luke 10:27

Because the Lord loves His Church and His creation, He wants to restore Kingdom values. This will bring healing to the Church, and then we can reach out to touch society. To bring wholeness to the Body, it is necessary for God to move, not only upon the individual believer, but also corporately, upon the whole Body of Christ in the different areas of human functioning — heart, soul, strength, mind and relationships. In order for us to become the loving community of believers God wants, we need to have a few adjustments take place. Some of those adjustments will come in the form of new structures which sovereignly come into place, while others will come through God's hand of correction.

The way God will go about doing this can be better understood by looking back at the Tabernacle of Moses, because God's way with the Church is first seen in the Tabernacle. It is a map for us to follow: *"Your way, O God, is in the sanctuary"* (Psalm 77:13, NKJ).

When Moses was building the Tabernacle in the wilderness, he did as God instructed and called for all the skilled craftsmen who had been given wisdom in their particular areas of gifting. Then the Lord said to Moses:

> *"See, I have chosen Bezalel son of Uri, the son of Hur, of the tribe of Judah, and I have filled him with the Spirit of God, with skill, ability and knowledge in all kinds of crafts."*
>
> Exodus 31:2-3

Moses said to the Israelites:

So Bezalel, Oholiab and every skilled person to whom the LORD *has given skill and ability to know how to carry out all the work of constructing the sanctuary are to do the work just as the Lord has commanded.*   Exodus 36:1

Bezalel was prepared by God and filled with His Spirit to accomplish his part in the task of building the Tabernacle in the wilderness for God's presence. Bezalel, then, represents the type of leader God calls. The Scriptures indicate that all the craftsmen who built the Tabernacle were skilled in their field and filled with wisdom, but they were also able to train others (see Exodus 35:34). As the Lord transforms our present Church structure, I sense Him saying that He will use people like Bezalel. They will be called forth from all walks of life and will be people whose skills encompass all of God's truth regarding science and nature. As a result, the Church's resources will be greatly expanded, and no group in society will be overlooked.

The type of knowledge and skills these new leaders have will be such that all the different areas of human functioning will be represented, so that we, as a Body, can come to wholeness. The extent to which we are not healed is the extent to which we hinder

the flow of God's Spirit through us and limit our
capacity to fill our positions in the Body of Christ.
A healthy Church is needed to bring in the end-time
harvest. The extent to which individual believers
have not filled their God-given positions in the Body
is the extent to which the Church is dysfunctional.
Paul tells us:

> *Now the body is not made up of one part but of*
> *many ... , so that there should be no division in*
> *the body, but that its parts should have equal*
> *concern for each other. If one part suffers, every*
> *part suffers with it; if one part is honored, every*
> *part rejoices with it. Now you are the body of*
> *Christ, and each one of you is a part of it.*
>   1 Corinthians 12:14 and 25-27

God has told us in both the Old and New Testa-
ments that all of His people have a part to play in
building His Kingdom on earth. We all have a place
and are individually important to God. We must learn
to lay hold of Him for ourselves so He can build us
into a mighty, powerful army. Jesus prayed for all
believers:

> *"My prayer is not for them alone. I pray also for*
> *those who will believe in me through their mes-*
> *sage, that all of them may be one, Father, just*

> *as you are in me and I am in you. May they*
> *also be in us so that the world may believe that*
> *you have sent me. I have given them the glory*
> *that you gave me, that they may be one as we*
> *are one: I in them and you in me. May they be*
> *brought to complete unity to let the world know*
> *that you sent me and have loved them even as*
> *you have loved me."*   John 17:20-23

The unity Jesus prays for will come as we are individually and corporately healed. The new apostolic leadership God will use to bring this healing will be people who have gone through a preparation process and who, as a result, are anointed by the Holy Spirit for the task. These people are not perfect, but have learned to put aside their own agendas in submission to God's will for their lives. These are the ones God will use to put His new structure in place because, like Bezalel, the Holy Spirit gives to them the blueprint for each of their different areas. I sense the Lord saying that these people will have the Church's best interests at heart, and their central desire will be to glorify God in all that they do.

These people will not come with wise and persuasive words, but with a demonstration of the Spirit's power, so that our faith will not rest on men's wisdom, but on God's power (see 1 Corinthians 2:4-5). These new leaders will model love, so that the Body

will, in turn, go out and love the community. I sense
the Holy Spirit saying that, aside from gifting, there
is only one qualification for apostolic leadership, and
that is to have learned unconditional love, to be per-
fected in love.

This group of people God has prepared is made up
of covenant keepers. God has tested them like he
tested Abraham, and they have given their firstfruits,
their best gifts to God.

Recently, a friend of mine, Anne, had a vision of
this new apostolic leadership. She saw a volcano with
hot lava flowing down the sides, killing everything
in its way. There were seeds buried in the ground
under the lava. Anne saw people emerging from a
river beside the volcano. The people wore white robes
and stepped from the river to receive garlands that
the Holy Spirit was giving to each one. Their flesh
had died in the fiery furnace of the volcano, but they
arose from the river to nurture life back into all the
seeds that were buried.

The meaning of this vision, as Anne was led to understand, was that the new leaders God is bringing
on the scene have been through the fire of affliction.
Their faith has been tested, and they have died to self-
ambition. They arise from the river of life. This
end-time remnant is made up of men and women
who will bring their firstfruits, their offerings and the
sacrifices of their lives and place them at the foot of

the cross, as a *Sweet Aroma* to God (see Ezekiel 20:40-41). These shepherds will gently lead the flock beside still waters. This is God's way of protecting the Body. Paul tells us to beware because there will be false apostles who masquerade as apostles of Christ and that we shouldn't be surprised by this because Satan himself masquerades as an angel of light (see 2 Corinthians 11:13-14).

As God was giving me understanding of these things, He reminded me of the vision of the orchestra (which I have described in Chapter Four) and also the dream of the staircase (in Chapter Ten). I received a greater depth of understanding regarding their meanings at this point in time. The different instruments in the orchestra represent the variety of giftings within the Body and how all of them are needed in order to play a symphony.

As the Lord was helping me to understand how He was raising up all these new skilled people to bring back Kingdom values, I sensed He was saying that the musicians in the orchestra were the new apostolic leadership. These people had spent much time practicing to play the right tune. They had spent much time learning to watch every cue from the Conductor. They had come to countless rehearsals.

A leader is someone who goes first. Leaders must first go through uncharted territory, find out the pitfalls and then show others the safest way to cross. I sense God is going to do something different and creative as He raises up the new leadership.

As the Spirit reminded me of this vision of the orchestra, I sensed He was saying that just as the Conductor had told some people to leave because they were unprepared, He was now saying that the time of preparation is finished. I sensed the Holy Spirit saying that the symphony is about to begin. God is about to play a melody which will enrapture the whole earth, and many will come to hear the beautiful sound.

At the same time, the Lord was showing me that there are some who have been in Christian leadership to date, but who will no longer be in leadership. This is because their training for this new move of God has been short-circuited. Paul asks the question:

> *You were running a good race. Who cut in on you and kept you from obeying the truth? That kind of persuasion does not come from the one who calls you.* Galatians 5:7-8

I sensed the Holy Spirit saying that not only individuals, but some churches and para-church organizations would cease to function because they have not kept in step with the Holy Spirit. They have become detached from the vine (see John 15:1-5).

I sensed, at the same time, that the Lord was saying

He has a company of believers who, like Joseph, have been prepared (out of sight) specifically for this time. Those who make up this remnant are waiting in the wings, and the Holy Spirit is about to bring them onto center stage.

As God was giving me understanding about these things, I also sensed some warnings. To understand these warnings, it is necessary to once again look back at the Tabernacle of Moses. When God gave Moses instructions to make the fragrant incense to burn upon the altar in the Holy Place, He said:

> *"Do not make any incense with this formula for yourselves; consider it holy to the* LORD. *Whoever makes any like it to enjoy its fragrance must be cut off from his people."* Exodus 30:37-38

The Altar of Incense was symbolic of prayer, praise, intercession and worship to Almighty God. The incense was burned upon the altar, and it released a fragrant aroma, which rose to God's throne. Worship is for God alone. No one and nothing must take His place, or such idolatry will be judged, as this passage shows.

In the Old Testament, we read that when David was bringing the Ark back to Jerusalem, Uzzah was struck dead by God, because he reached out to steady the Ark when the oxen stumbled. The Scriptures tell us,

"The LORD*'s anger burned against Uzzah because of his irreverent act; therefore God struck him down and he died there beside the ark of God"* (2 Samuel 6:7). Uzzah's action stemmed from ignorance, but he was still judged by God and suffered the consequences. The Ark represented God's presence, and no one was to carry the Ark except the Levites — God's designated ministers. David was presumptuous in not following God's specific command and in allowing Uzzah to take over the work assigned to others. He failed to protect Uzzah from his own ignorant zeal.

As the Lord reminded me of the story of Uzzah, it became clear that this is what He was showing me in the dream of the staircase described in Chapter Ten. The Christians who were leaping through the hole in the wall and down the steep embankment were ignorant of God's ways. They did not understand the progressive steps of training in righteousness that the Lord takes us through before bringing us to our destination in Him. They injured themselves by going places they were not called to by God, their presumption having moved them outside His protection.

Those commissioned by God to build up the Church for works of service are responsible for mending the hole in the wall by teaching God's ways through His Word. It seems God is saying that He is about to bring correction, that His judgment is about to come upon the Church for the sin of presumption, because men have placed themselves where God has not placed them and taken upon themselves tasks He has not assigned them. Presumption is taking God for granted, which leaves us wide open to spiritual attack, for it is the fear of God which keeps us safe. It is necessary for the fear of God to come back into the Church in order for us to be restored.

In the New Testament, we read of Ananias and Sapphira, who also were presumptuous, and they fell down dead after lying to the Holy Spirit (see Acts 5:1-10). God demands that His holiness be respected in the Church. The Lord did not show me specifically how He would deal with people who placed themselves in self-appointed positions, except to show me that they would be stopped. In the dream of the staircase, I saw many Christians who were disabled by their injuries.

There is another group of Christians that I believe the Lord has spoken to me about, and it is made up of Christians who are appointed by God to various roles within the Church. To give me understanding of what He intends to do, the Lord led me to read again the story of the tower of Babel:

> *They said, "Come, let us build ourselves a city, with a tower that reaches to the heavens, so that we may make a name for ourselves and not be scattered over the face of the whole earth."*

But the L<small>ORD</small> came down to see the city and the
tower that the men were building. The L<small>ORD</small>
said, "If as one people speaking the same lan-
guage they have begun to do this, then nothing
they plan to do will be impossible for them.
Come, let us go down and confuse their lan-
guage so they will not understand each other."

Genesis 11:4-7

I was given to understand that if those whom God has appointed to various works of service are not speaking what the Holy Spirit wants them to say, then the Spirit will confuse their speech so they are unable to continue. This is to prevent believers from building an empire unto themselves and to prevent the Church from being led astray. I believe unrepented sin in the lives of Christians will also be exposed so that God can heal the Church and bring her to holiness.

In regard to when and how these things will occur, I sensed the Lord say three things. A few days before He began to give me understanding of these issues, I woke up in the early hours of the morning and sensed the Holy Spirit say, "I'm about to release the fragrance; I'm about to break open the spikenard." When I asked the Lord what fragrance He was referring to, He did not answer right away. The understanding came several days later as the Holy Spirit was showing me where the new apostolic leaders were coming from. I believe the fragrance the Lord is referring to is this new company of believers He has prepared.

When Mary broke open the alabaster jar of expensive perfume made of pure nard, she poured it on the body of Jesus to anoint Him for burial (see Mark 14:3-9). In some way, I sensed the Holy Spirit was saying that the release of the fragrance of these people who have prepared themselves for this next move of God will act like an anointing for burial of the old Church structure.

I sensed the Lord saying the release of these new apostolic people will be like a blossoming tree in spring. We go out one morning, and there is the first blossom. The next day, there are a few more blossoms, and then gradually there is an abundance of blossoms ... until the whole world is filled with their fragrance. The fragrance emitted by these blossoms is the love of God through Jesus Christ. And the reason their presence acts as an anointing for burial of the old Church structure is that love conquers all; it endures where everything else fails; love overcomes; it is the greatest of virtues (see 1 Corinthians 13:7).

The second thing I sensed the Lord say was that bringing back biblical values means turning the Church upside down. It seemed that He was saying He would begin with: *"the last will be first, and the first will be last"* (Matthew 20:16). This refers to many things at many levels, I believe, not only people, but beliefs, things, ways and even nations. In helping me understand what He intends to do, the Lord reminded me of Luke 10:27 and its importance in this new apostolic reformation. God will be restoring His truths to us in the five areas of human functioning: spiritual, emotional, physical, intellectual and social.

I sensed the Holy Spirit say that the first area to be restored would be the area of the mind. When I questioned the Lord about the large percentage within the Church who have never moved beyond their intellects to the spiritual, He quickly corrected me. God is not referring to worldly wisdom here, but rather, I believe, He is referring to harnessing the enormous intellectual resources available in the Body. There are several reasons for this. First, God loves us and wants us whole in every way, so we can enjoy life. Second, seeing the vast expanse of knowledge God has given us will cause us to magnify His excellent greatness and glorify Him even more. Third, these new creative ideas will equip us to fulfill the Great Commission.

While God intends to bless us with the richness of the diversity of gifts He has placed in our midst, He also intends to deal with the sin of presumption — to cause us to see how much we need one another. The fear of God will come upon us as we realize we cannot take God for granted, and we will develop a humility regarding His holiness and His transcendent greatness.

When the Lord had finished showing me all these things, I was surprised by what He did next. Three days later, I woke in the early hours of the morning to hear a gentle whisper: "I cannot heal the corporate mind of the Church until I am invited." I responded, as a representative of the Body of Christ, by laying down our corporate mind at the foot of the cross as firstfruits for restoration.

In the section God's Numbering System, I mentioned the symbolic way God uses numbers. I thought I had finished looking up symbolic numbers, but once again I felt prompted by the Spirit to take note of when He spoke to me. When I worked it out, I realized it was the sixth day of the sixth month at 5 AM. Six is the number of man. That it occurs twice is significant, as two is the number of witness. Five is the number of grace. God is gracious to warn us of the things He is about to do.

The third thing I sensed the Holy Spirit saying, in relation to all these things, was: "Let the sound go out! Let the sound be clear!"

Finally, a scripture the Lord has laid on my heart:

> "I counsel you to buy from me gold refined in the fire, so you can become rich; and white clothes to wear, so you can cover your shameful nakedness; and salve to put on your eyes, so you can see."   Revelation 3:18

An Invitation

If you have never accepted Jesus Christ as your Lord and Savior, if you are unsure or if you once knew Him but wandered away and now feel the need to recommit your life to Him, you can do so by praying this prayer:

Father in Heaven,

Thank You for sending Your Son, Jesus Christ, to die on the cross for my sins. I admit I am a sinner. I have lived my own way, independently of You. I have not followed Your principles, but now I want to learn how to please You. Lord Jesus, come into my heart, forgive my sin and take control of my life.

Thank You for the precious gift of salvation.

In the name of Jesus Christ, I pray,
Amen!

If you desire to have the same power that came upon the disciples at Pentecost, you can have it by praying this prayer:

Father in Heaven,

Your Word says, in Acts 1:8, that we shall receive power when the Holy Spirit comes upon us. I ask You now for the Holy Spirit to come in power, to saturate me in His presence, so that I might share the message of salvation with boldness, that I might be a powerful witness for my Savior Jesus and that the gifts of the Spirit might be released in my life for the purpose of effective and fruitful ministry.

I receive by faith. Thank You.

In Jesus' name,
Amen!

Endnotes

God's Numbering System

1. John J. Davis, Biblical Numerology, Baker Book House, (Grand Rapids, MI: 1968) p. 104
2. Kevin J. Connor, *Interpreting the Symbols and Types*, Bible Temple Publishing, Portland, Oregon, 1980, p.55.
3. Ibid., p.53.
4. Ibid., p.55.
5. Ibid., p.54.
6. Ibid.
7. Ibid., p.53.

Chapter Two

1. Anne H. Soukhanov, ed., *Encarta World English Dictionary*, St. Martin's Press, New York, 1999, p.1377.

Chapter Three

1. Brian Fay, *Critical Social Science*, Cornell University Press, New York, 1987, p.11.
2. E.W. Kenyon, *The Blood Covenant*, Kenyon's Gospel Publishing Society, 1995, p.6.
3. H. Clay Trumbull, *The Blood Covenant*, Impact Books, Kirkwood, Missouri, 1975, p.148.
4. E.W. Kenyon, p.8.
5. Ibid., p.11.
6. Kevin Connor and Ken Malmin, *The Covenants*, K.J.C. Publications, Blackburn South, Victoria, Australia, 1983, p.11.
7. Craig Hill, *The Blood Covenant* tape series, Family Foundations Int'l., Littleton, Colorado, Tape I.
8. Ibid.
9. Ibid.

Chapter Four

1. Kenneth S. Wuest, *Wuest's Word Studies From the Greek New Testament*, William B. Eerdmans Publishing Company, Grand Rapids,

Michigan, 1973, Vol. 1, p.162.

2. See Kevin J. Connor, *The Tabernacle of Moses*, Acacia Press Pty Ltd, Blackburn, Victoria, Australia, 1975.

3. M.R. De Haan, *The Tabernacle*, Zondervan Publishing House, Grand Rapids, Michigan, 1955, p.84.

4. Ibid., p.98.

5. Ibid., p.104.

6. Ibid., p.120.

7. Donald C. Stamps, ed., *The Full Life Study Bible*, Zondervan Publishing House, Grand Rapids, Michigan, 1992) p.1654.

8. Oswald Chambers, *Still Higher for the Highest*, Oswald Chambers Publications Association and Marshall Morgan and Scott Marshall Pickering, Bastertoke, Hands, UK, 1970, p.26.

9. Paul Billheimer, *Don't Waste Your Sorrows*, Christian Literature Crusade, Fort Washington, Pennsylvania, 1977, p.8.

10. Martin Luther, *The Oxford Dictionary of Quotations*, Oxford University Press, Oxford, 1979, p.320.

11. Oswald Chambers, Still Higher for His Highest, Zondervan Publishing House (Grand Rapids, MI: 1990) p.174.

Chapter Five

1. Donald C. Stamps, ed., *The Full Life Study Bible*, Zondervan Publishing House, Grand Rapids, Michigan, 1992, p.1431.

2. Joseph A. Fitzmyer, *The Gospel According to Luke x-xxiv*, The Anchor Bible, Doubleday, New York, 1985, p.880.

3. Ibid.

4. Ibid.

5. Ibid.

6. Anne H. Soukhanov, ed., *Encarta World English Dictionary*, St. Martin's Press, New York, 1999, p.699.

Chapter Six

1. R.T. Kendall, *God Meant It For Good*. Morning Star Publications, Charlotte, North Carolina, 1986, p.72.

2. Jedediah Tham, *The Three Conditions of Life*, tape series, Resurrection Life Ministries, Queensland, Australia, 1998, Tape 5.

3. Kenneth S. Wuest, *Wuest's Word Studies From the Greek New Testament*, William B. Eerdman's Publishing Company, Grand Rapids, Michigan, 1955, Vol. 1, p.134.

4. Jedediah Tham.

5. Kenneth S. Wuest, p.134.

6. Jedediah Tham.

7. Ibid.

8. W. Phillip Keller, *Joshua*, Kregal Publications, Grand Rapids, Michigan, 1992, p.63.

Chapter Seven

1. Walter A. Elwell, ed., *Evangelical Commentary on the Bible*, Baker Book House, Grand Rapids, Michigan, 1989, p.587.
2. See Wesley Campbell, *Welcoming a Visitation of the Holy Spirit*, Creation House, Altamonte Springs, Florida, 1996.
3. Ruth Ward Helfin, *Golden Glory*, McDougal Publishing, Hagerstown, Maryland, 2000.
4. Ibid.
5. M.R. De Haan, *The Tabernacle*, Zondervan Publishing House, Grand Rapids, Michigan, 1955, p.95.

Chapter Ten

1. Kevin J. Connor, *Interpreting the Symbols and Types*, Bible Temple Publishing, Portland, Oregon, 1992, p.171.
2. Ibid., p.178.

Chapter Eleven

1. Kevin J. Connor, *The Tabernacle of Moses*, Acacia Press Pty Ltd, Blackburn, Victoria, Australia, 1975, pp.47-51.
2. John I. Durham, *Word Biblical Commentary*, Word Books Publisher, Waco, Texas, 1987, Vol. 3, p.408.
3. Frank E. Gabelein, ed., *The Expositors Bible Commentary*, Zondervan Publishing House, Grand Rapids, Michigan, 1990, Vol. 2, p.453.
4. Jerome H. Smith, ed., *The New Treasury of Scripture Knowledge*, Thomas Nelson Publishers, Nashville, Tennessee, 1992, p.120.
5. Lori Wilke, *The Costly Anointing*, Destiny Image Publishers, Shippensburg, Pennsylvania, 1991, p.29.
6. Kevin J. Connor, p.51.
7. Notes on Arthur Stace were taken from information supplied by St. Barnabas Church of England, The Broadway, Sydney, N.S.W.

Chapter Twelve

1. Bill Hamon, *Prophets and the Prophetic Movement*, Destiny Image Publishers, Shippensburg, Pennsylvania, 1990, p.45.
2. C. Peter Wagner, ed., *The New Apostolic Churches*, Regal Books, Ventura, California, 1998, p.18.
3. Ibid, p.18-19.
4. Phil Marshall, "The Rise and Rise of the Apostles," *Renewal Journal*, School of Ministries of Brisbane Christian Outreach Centre, Issue 13, 1999/1, p.29.
5. Bill Hamon, p.153.

To contact the author:

Liz Todd
Access Outreach Australia
P.O. Box 4092
Eight Mile Plains
Brisbane, Queensland
Australia 4113

Fax: (07) 3843 3815

— *Notes* —

— *Notes* —

— *Notes* —

— *Notes* —